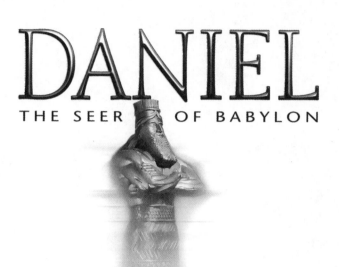

DANIEL

THE SEER OF BABYLON

To order additional copies of *Daniel: The Seer of Babylon,* by Gerhard Pfandl, call 1-800-765-6955.

Visit us at www.reviewandherald.com for information on other Review and Herald® products.

DANIEL

THE SEER OF BABYLON

Gehard Pfandl

REVIEW AND HERALD® PUBLISHING ASSOCIATION
HAGERSTOWN, MD 21740

This book was
Edited by Gerald Wheeler
Copyedited by Delma Miller and James Cavil
Cover designed by PierceCreative
Cover art by Lars Justinen/Justinen Creative Group
Typeset: 11/13 Bembo

PRINTED IN U.S.A.

08 07 06 05 04   5 4 3 2 1

R&H Cataloging Service
Pfandl, Gerhard, 1943-
     Daniel: the seer of Babylon.

     1. Bible. O.T. Daniel—Study and Teaching.
I. Title.

          224.5

ISBN 0-8280-1829-4

Dedication

For my wife, Maureen,
and our sons, Steve and Robert

Contents

Introduction

The book of Daniel is the shortest of the four major prophets. Yet for Seventh-day Adventists it is the most important and most frequently studied book of the 16 major and minor prophets in the Old Testament. It records certain historical events in the life of Daniel and a number of dreams and visions given to the prophet and to Nebuchadnezzar, the king of Babylon.

Daniel contains timeless truths just as relevant today as when first written 2,500 years ago, and we do well to pay close attention to them. Ellen White repeatedly called attention to the study of the book of Daniel: "As we near the close of this world's history," she wrote, "the prophecies recorded by Daniel demand our special attention, as they relate to the very time in which we are living."[1]

Not only do we need to understand the prophecies recorded in Daniel, but studying them, she says, does something for our spiritual life. "When the books of Daniel and Revelation are better understood, believers will have an entirely different religious experience. They will be given such glimpses of the open gates of heaven that heart and mind will be impressed with the character that all must develop in order to realize the blessedness which is to be the reward of the pure in heart."[2]

The book of Daniel belongs to what scholars call apocalyptic literature. The term *apocalyptic* comes from the Greek *apokalypsis,* meaning "an unveiling" or "a revelation." The biblical apocalyptic books of Daniel and Revelation describe by means of symbolic visions the course of human history and the final advent of the kingdom of God.

The book divides into two parts: the first six chapters contain primarily history; the last six chapters, mostly visions. The climax in each narrative is the elevation of the worshipers of the true God, and each vision ends in the establishment of the kingdom of God. The first chapter tells the story of the destruction of God's earthly kingdom, Judah. The last chapter promises the deliverance of the people of God in the time of the end and the inheritance of the heavenly kingdom that will last forever.

Daniel, in his youth as well as in his old age, was a man of unusual courage and faith. He never compromised his conviction, and at every stage in life he maintained his trust in God regardless of the circumstances. Whether the issue was personal advancement or death in a lions' den, he remained firm in his decisions and fully committed to his God. He was truly "a man for all seasons."

Many Old Testament scholars believe that an unknown Jew around 165 B.C. wrote most of the book of Daniel to comfort and bring hope to the Jews who at that time were being persecuted by the Seleucid king Antiochus IV Epiphanes. Conservative scholars, including Seventh-day Adventists, continue to hold that the prophet Daniel composed the book in the sixth century B.C. and that it contains true prophecies. The claims of the book itself (Dan. 7:1, 2, 15; 8:1; 9:2; 10:2; 12:4, 5), the testimony of Jesus (Matt. 24:15), as well as the witness of Josephus, a Jewish historian who died about A.D. 100, all support this position. Furthermore, only someone living in the sixth century B.C. could have known some of the historical facts found in the book. The knowledge of such facts soon disappeared after the sixth century B.C., and scholars have recovered them only in recent times through archaeological discoveries.

Manuscript discoveries at Qumran have demonstrated the popularity of Daniel among the people there and testify to the way in which Jews revered and cited Daniel as Scripture in the second century B.C., an approval difficult to understand if the book had been written only in the second century B.C. There would not have been enough time for the book to be circulated, venerated, and accepted as canonical Scripture.

The name Daniel means "God is my judge," and the pages of the book elaborate that truth. The book begins and ends with references to judgment, at the beginning apostate Israel (Dan. 1:1, 2) and at the end the king of the north (Dan. 11:40-12:2). The middle of the book (Dan. 7:9-13) portrays God as the Ancient of Days with the books of judgment open and the multitudes of angels present. On each side of this great judgment scene we find further references to judgment. In chapter 4 heaven judges Nebuchadnezzar, the proud boaster, and humbles him to animal status, and in chapter 5 Belshazzar, his grandson, receives the message: "You have been weighed in the balances, and found wanting." Chapters 8 and 9 indicate the beginning date of the judgment to come, and the twelfth chapter spells out in detail its significance concerning rewards and punishments.

The historical chapters of the book (1-6) illustrate how God vindicates and delivers those who remain faithful in the midst of pagan nations. These chapters contain the motif of trial and trouble ending in elevation and glory. Thus the book continually proclaims the good news that trials and temptations are followed by blessings for those obedient to God. It is a message that people still need to hear and believe today.

---

[1] Ellen G. White, *Prophets and Kings* (Boise, Idaho: Pacific Press Pub. Assn., 1957), p. 547.

[2] White, *Testimonies to Ministers* (Mountain View, Calif.: Pacific Press Pub. Assn., 1962), p. 114.

CHAPTER 1

"To Eat or Not to Eat"— That Is the Question

The opening chapter of Daniel introduces us to the four heroes of the book: Daniel, the main character of the book, and his three friends Hananiah, Mishael, and Azariah. The book says nothing of their parents, but few individuals have become great and good without the instructions received at a parent's knee. Taken captive to Babylon, the four individuals came under pressure to conform to the customs of the Babylonians, but they remained true to their God, and He rewarded them with exceptional wisdom and insight. By their commitment to God and faith in Him they became examples for all Christians who today may face the temptation to compromise their faith to keep a job or to be accepted by others.

Information

A prison chaplain on his rounds through the large prison compound noticed one of the inmates sewing a patch of cloth on an old garment. Greeting the man cheerfully, he said, "Good morning, my friend! Sewing today?"

"No, Chaplain," the man replied with a sad face, "reaping!"

As the book of Daniel opens, the southern kingdom of Judah is reaping a bitter harvest for its long years of disobedience to God (2 Kings 21:10-16; 24:18-20). Justice, it is said, travels with leaden feet, giving the sinner time to repent. In the case of Israel, the Lord intended that His people should be a light to the Gentiles (Isa. 42:6), but their continued apostasy eventually led to their destruction as Jeremiah had predicted (Jer. 25:8, 9).

At the end of the seventh century B.C. the kingdom of Babylon replaced the Assyrians as the dominant power in the ancient Near East. Joining forces with the Medes from northern Iran, the Babylonians defeated the Assyrians, capturing the city of Asshur in 614 B.C. and sacking Nineveh in 612 B.C.

Expanding their empire to the west, the Babylonians encountered the

DANIEL

Egyptians at Carchemish on the upper Euphrates River in 605 B.C. According to Jeremiah 46:1-12 Nebuchadnezzar and his Babylonian forces soundly defeated Pharaoh Necho at Carchemish. The battle changed the political landscape in the ancient Near East as what had formerly been under Egyptian control now fell to the Babylonians, including the kingdom of Judah.

Josiah, the last good king of Judah, died in 609 B.C. His son Jehoiakim was an Egyptian vassal until Nebuchadnezzar in 605 B.C. forced him to submit to Babylon. When Jehoiakim revolted against Babylon in 598 B.C. Nebuchadnezzar personally led his army against Jerusalem and conquered it in 597 B.C. He took the new king Jehoiachin, the son of Jehoiakim, who had been on the throne for barely three months, to Babylon and installed Jehoiakim's brother Zedekiah as ruler. At the same time Nebuchadnezzar confiscated a large quantity of Temple utensils and took 10,000 captives, among them the prophet Ezekiel (2 Kings 24:10-16; Eze. 1:1).

A number of years later Zedekiah made an alliance with Egypt against Babylon (Jer. 37:7, 8). Not willing to lose any of his western possessions to Egypt, Nebuchadnezzar marched against Judah, devastated the whole land, and in 586 B.C. captured Jerusalem and burned it to the ground (2 Kings 25:9, 10).

Explanation

The book of Daniel opens with two brief statements concerning the Babylonian king's siege of Jerusalem in 605 B.C.: "Nebuchadnezzar king of Babylon came to Jerusalem and besieged it. And the Lord gave Jehoiakim king of Judah into his hand" (verses 1, 2). The first statement describes the event in terms of secular history; the second supplies the event's spiritual dimension. Throughout the book we find these two perspectives of history interwoven and revealed. Particularly in the first six chapters of the book the spiritual dimension provides the explanation for the historical events.

Jerusalem and Babylon (Dan. 1:1)—The book of Daniel, like the rest of Scripture, is the story of two cities: Jerusalem and Babylon. One represents the rule of righteousness, the other the reign of wickedness. Jerusalem reveals the mystery of godliness, Babylon the mystery of sin. The first time we read of Babylon and Jerusalem in Scripture is in the book of Genesis (Gen. 11 and 14), while the last time we hear of them is in the book of Revelation (Rev. 18 and 21). The stories and prophecies of the book of Daniel illustrate the principles of the ancient conflict between good and evil.

14

Babylon Conquers Jerusalem (Dan. 1:1, 2)—Daniel 1:1 says that Nebuchadnezzar came to Jerusalem "in the third year of . . . Jehoiakim." According to Jeremiah 25:1, Nebuchadnezzar besieged Jerusalem in the fourth year of Jehoiakim. We can resolve the seeming discrepancy when we recognize that the ancient Near East employed two systems of dating at that time, both found in the Old Testament. The accession-year method used by Daniel counted the year when a king came to the throne as his accession year, and the next full year as his first year. The nonaccession-year method used in the book of Jeremiah counted the year when a king began to reign as his first year, even though it may have lasted only a few weeks or months. The following diagram illustrates the two approaches:

Accession-year method:
   Daniel 1:1: Accession year, first year, second year, third year

Nonaccession-year method:
   Jeremiah 25:1: First year, second year, third year, fourth year

Training for Service (Dan. 1:3-7)—King Nebuchadnezzar instructed Ashpenaz, one of his officers, to select the most promising among the exiled youth and to train them in Babylonian culture. Many years earlier, the prophet Isaiah told King Hezekiah that some of his descendants would become "eunuchs in the palace of the king of Babylon" (Isa. 39:7). Rabbinic tradition, therefore, asserts that Daniel and his three friends were descendants of king Hezekiah[1] who were made into eunuchs at the court of Babylon.[2] The word *sarîs* (eunuch), however, can simply refer to a high officer of the court. For example, Genesis 39:1 calls Potiphar a *sarîs* even though he was married.

Nebuchadnezzar, it seems, intended to train the cream of the crop of young Jews for future service in his kingdom. To keep distant lands subjugated could be costly for his army. What better way than to give the sons of the conquered nobility and intelligentsia a thorough Babylonian education and training, and then either send them back to administer their own homeland for him, or let them serve him at the court in Babylon. The Romans later would also take royal hostages and educate them in Rome with the idea that they would be friends of Rome when they returned to their native land.

15

The young Hebrews were to learn "the language and literature of the Chaldeans" (Dan. 1:4). The "language" most likely included (1) Akkadian, the native language of the Babylonians; (2) Sumerian, the ancient language of Sumer used in their religious practices and for their technical literature; and (3) Aramaic, the language of international commerce and diplomacy. Akkadian and Sumerian were written in the difficult cuneiform script that was best suited for inscribing clay tablets. The literature of the Chaldeans, whose name became a byword for "magician" or "diviner," included the study of sexagesimal mathematics (based on units of six), for which the Babylonians were famous in history, and astronomy. However, their curriculum most likely included also the study of astrology and the art of divination or reading omens, practices severely condemned in the Old Testament (Deut. 18:10). Whether they somehow managed to avoid these subjects, we do not know. What we do know is that through a consistent prayerful dependence on God they were able to escape the corrupting influences of their studies. "Daniel was subjected to the severest temptations that can assail the youth of today; yet he was true to the religious instruction received in early life. . . . Prayer was to him a necessity. He made God his strength, and the fear of God was continually before him in all the transactions of his life."[3]

Part of the Babylonian reeducation program included a change of names. Daniel ("God is my judge") now went by Belteshazzar (probably "Bel protect his life"), Hananiah ("Yahweh has been gracious") became Shadrach (the meaning is uncertain, possibly "command of Aku," the moon god); Mishael ("who is like God?") was changed to Meshach (perhaps "who is what Aku is?"); and Azariah ("Yahweh helps") was called Abednego (a distortion of "servant of Nebo," one of the two principal gods of Babylon).

In Western culture, where the meaning of names is not very important, the change of names may seem insignificant. In the ancient Near East, however, names and their connotation formed part of a person's identity. Thus the Babylonians began the process of reeducation by obliterating any reference to the Hebrew God and substituting names containing allusions or references to Babylonian gods. Nebuchadnezzar "did not compel the Hebrew youth to renounce their faith in favor of idolatry, but he hoped to bring this about gradually."[4]

A Test of Loyalty (Dan. 1:8-16)—Daniel and his three friends could not change what others called them, but when it came to eating the best food their captors could offer, they declined. Their reason was not just because some of the food was most likely unclean, but also because it had been offered to idols before it was served. A Babylonian royal meal began with an act of pagan worship, and those who participated in the meal considered themselves as having taken part in the religious rite. Daniel and his friends, therefore, requested to be excused from the king's table. They would not act contrary to God's will, and they refused to violate their conscience.

The decision of the four young Hebrews to reject the king's food was a courageous act. The royal court could have regarded it as an insult to the king and as evidence of subordination. The pressure to conform must have been intense. No doubt other Jewish young men laughed at their sensitivity. Away from home, away from the gaze of parents and elders, why worry about the king's food? However, Daniel, as spokesman for his friends, refused to give in. First, he went to the chief official and asked his permission to abstain from the king's food. When the court official refused to participate in their plan, Daniel went to his subordinate, the steward, and proposed a brief 10-day test (verses 12, 13). The determination of the young men may indicate that they were in the habit of turning away from evil. Habits form as people make repeated decisions and then act in response to them. Such habits comprise a person's character, and character determines eternal destiny.

Contrary to what some may think, Daniel and his friends did not live off beans and peas or salads for the next three years. The word zer'onîm, translated "pulse" (KJV) or "vegetable" (NKJV), refers to "things that are sown." It would include all the grains that could be made into many a savory dish as well as bread.

Was the diet Daniel requested really adequate? "A number of dietary studies have demonstrated the nutritional adequacy of the lacto-ovo and the pure vegetarian diets in adults as well as in adolescents and pregnant women. . . . There is less obesity among vegetarians and some statistics indicate there is less heart disease. Incidence of heart disease among Seventh-day Adventist men who are lacto-ovovegetarians is only 60 percent as high as among average California men, and the age of incidence is a full decade later."[5]

Daniel's faith in the matter was remarkable. He was confident that in only 10 days God would bring about such a change in their appearance that it would convince the steward to alter their diet permanently. The outcome of the test, of course, vindicated the Hebrew captive. God honored the faith of the young men and performed a miracle. At the end of the 10 days the four young Hebrews looked better and healthier than those who ate from the king's table.

God Honors Faithfulness (Dan. 1:17-21)—Daniel and his friends excelled in the various fields of study, for "God gave them knowledge and skill in all literature and wisdom" (verse 17). It illustrates the truth the man of God had said to Eli many years before: "Those who honor Me I will honor" (1 Sam. 2:30). Even as the Babylonians forced them to undertake a process of assimilation, the true source of their wisdom was not the Chaldean curriculum, but the God of Israel.

Daniel's special gift was the ability to understand visions and dreams, as had Joseph in the book of Genesis. In the first half of the book of Daniel he interprets dreams for others, while in the second half he receives the visions and dreams himself. The prophet might well have prayed with the psalmist, "You, through Your commandments, make me wiser than my enemies; for they are ever with me. I have more understanding than all my teachers, for Your testimonies are my meditation. I understand more than the ancients, because I keep Your precepts" (Ps. 119:98-100).

At the end of the three-year course the Hebrew captives had their final exam. As in British universities in times past, the final test, it seems, was oral, not written. Nebuchadnezzar personally evaluated them, and he found Daniel and his friends 10 times better than all the other students, hence he had them selected to serve him (Dan. 1:19). Subsequently, when he had occasion to consult them, he found them even better than all the magicians and astrologers in his realm (verse 20).

Success in this first test prepared them for the temptations and trials that lay ahead. What if they had failed? They would most likely have succumbed to the greater tests in chapters 3 and 6. By remaining firm in their first challenge, they gained experience that helped them in the future.

Application

What can we learn from the experience of the four young Hebrews?

1. God Is in Control.—Perhaps the first lesson we can take away from this chapter is that in spite of appearances to the contrary, God is in control of history. From a human perspective, Nebuchadnezzar was the great victor. He conquered Jerusalem, looted the Temple that Solomon had built, and forced thousands of the people into captivity. The Bible, however, takes us behind the scenes and shows us that the Lord was in control all along. God is sovereign and directs the world by His providence. While He gave Jerusalem into the hands of Nebuchadnezzar (Dan. 1:2), he also gave knowledge and skill to the four young Hebrews (verse 17).

2. Tests of Character Are Opportunities to Grow.—At the

very outset of their time in Babylon there came a decisive test of character to all the young Hebrew captives at the king's court. Sadly, as far as we know, only four of them declined the food offered to idols. They knew it could have serious consequences for them, even the loss of life, but God's approval was more important than the favor of the most powerful king on earth. "In reaching this decision, the Hebrew youth did not act presumptuously, but in firm reliance upon God. They did not choose to be singular, but they would be so rather than dishonor God. Should they compromise with wrong in this instance by yielding to the pressure of circumstances, their departure from principle would weaken their sense of right and their abhorrence of wrong. The first wrong step would lead to others, until, their connection with Heaven severed, they would be swept away by temptation."[6] Frequently we see trials and temptations as personal nightmares, yet God uses them to give formation, direction, and character to our lives. No car, boat, or plane is fit for use unless it has undergone testing. The same is true of the citizens of God's kingdom.

3. Christians Must Stand Up for What They Believe.—Daniel and his friends found themselves seized from the shadows of the Jerusalem Temple and forced to live in a strange land where idol worship was part of life. Yet they were willing to resist the dominant culture of their day. They were willing to stand up for what they believed. As Christians today, we too live in a strange land, surrounded by a culture hostile toward most basic Christian values. The god of modern culture is not the God of the Bible but the god of self. "Personal gratification and self-realization are prized over any sense of the other person, any sense of community, whether that community is the family, the church, the city, the nation, or the global community."[7] All believers, therefore, have to ask themselves, "Who am I?" or more important, "Whose am I? Do I belong to the Lord? And if so, how am I to relate to the culture in which I live?" Jesus sends us into the world (John 17:18), yet He calls us not to be of the world (verse 14), and Paul challenges us not to be "conformed to the world" (Rom. 12:2). Like Daniel, every Christian must interact with the surrounding culture, yet they must also know when it is time to stand against it.

[1] J. Braverman, *Jerome's Commentary on Daniel: A Study of Comparative Jewish and Christian Interpretations of the Hebrew Bible,* Catholic Biblical Quarterly Monograph Series (Washington, D.C.: Catholic Bible Association of America, 1978), vol. 7, pp. 67, 68.
[2] Louis Ginzberg, *The Legends of the Jews* (New York: Jewish Publication Society, 1910-1938), vol. 4, p. 326, and vol. 6, p. 415.

³ Ellen G. White, *Fundamentals of Christian Education* (Nashville: Southern Pub. Assn., 1923), p. 78.

⁴ White, *Prophets and Kings,* p. 481.

⁵ Marian Arlin, *The Science of Nutrition,* 2nd ed. (New York: Macmillan Pub. Co., 1977), p. 96.

⁶ White, *Prophets and Kings,* p. 483.

⁷ Tremper Longman III, *Daniel,* The NIV Application Commentary (Grand Rapids: Zondervan, 1999), p. 62.

CHAPTER 2

Nebuchadnezzar's Image

Nebuchadnezzar's dream of a great image and Daniel's inspired explanation offer fundamental evidence for the inspiration of Scripture. In 184 Hebrew words Daniel describes the course of history from his day until the end of time, and thereby provides comfort to God's people by assuring them that when the great empires of the world have run their course the kingdom of the Messiah shall overthrow them all and establish the everlasting kingdom of God.

Information

Daniel 2 opens with a chronological puzzle. Verse 1 states that Nebuchadnezzar had the dream in his second year, whereas chapter 1 tells us that the training of Daniel and his friends lasted for three years (Dan. 1:5). Since the four Hebrew captives, at the end of the chapter, get promoted to leadership positions, their educational period seems to have come to an end. The puzzle can be solved if we follow E. J. Young's suggestion that it started in Nebuchadnezzar's accession year and that we count the three years according to the principle of inclusive reckoning, which regards part of a year as a whole year.[1]

Years of Daniel's Training	Nebuchadnezzar's Years
First year	Year of accession
Second year	First year
Third year	Second year

The Aramaic Language—The second chapter introduces us to the Aramaic language that the book of Daniel uses from Daniel 2:4 until the end of chapter 7. In chapter 8 Daniel reverts back to Hebrew. The Aramaeans of northern Syria and northwestern Mesopotamia spoke Aramaic, a Semitic language closely related to Hebrew. Although the Aramaean states lost their independence when the Assyrians conquered their territories in the eighth century B.C., the Aramaic language itself slowly spread throughout the ancient Near East and replaced Akkadian as the language of commerce and diplomacy in the Babylonian and Persian empires.

Why did Daniel write half of his book in Aramaic and the other half in Hebrew? We know he began writing in Aramaic at the point where the Chaldeans addressed the king in Aramaic (Dan. 2:4). Perhaps he continued with Aramaic until he finished that day. When he resumed writing (Dan. 8:1), at a later date, he reverted to Hebrew.

Dreams—Because people in the ancient world regarded dreams as revelations from the gods, royal courts in Mesopotamia and Egypt had professional dream interpreters. People often slept near temples or holy places in the hope of receiving a dream from their gods. Possibly, because of the Babylonian preoccupation with dreams, God chose this means to communicate with Nebuchadnezzar.

Chaldeans—Originally the word referred to a group of tribes in Lower Mesopotamia who founded the Neo-Babylonian Empire. Eventually the whole of Babylonia received the name Chaldea (Jer. 50:10; 51:24). In the book of Daniel the ethnic name has become a designation for royal counselors who functioned as priests. "The term Chaldeans in this sense is found not only in Daniel but also in the works of Herodotus, Strabo, and Diodorus Siculus, and in Palmyrene inscriptions."[2]

Four Metals—The four-metal symbolism existed in the ancient world long before Daniel's time. The Greek poet Hesiod (c. 800 B.C.) in his book *Works and Days* employed gold, silver, bronze, and iron to represent eras in human history. However, significant differences do exist between the book of Daniel and Hesiod's work: 1. Hesiod inserted an Age of Heroes between the Bronze and the Iron ages. Thus he arrived "at five ages between the time of man's innocence and his own day: gold, silver, bronze, the age of heroes, iron."[3] 2. In Hesiod's work we have a sequence of five transient empires; in Daniel 2 a fifth empire of eternal duration follows the four world ones. 3. Hesiod's predictions do not lead to an eschatological climax, while in Daniel 2 everything builds up to it.

Some interpreters have concluded that Daniel 2 depends on Hesiod's scheme of four world empires. G. F. Hasel, however, suggests that the correspondence between Hesiod and Daniel 2 most likely reflects a common tradition that both Hesiod and God in Daniel 2 "appropriated each in their own ways."[4]

Explanation

The Crisis at Nebuchadnezzar's Palace (Dan. 2:1-13)—Contemplating the future of his kingdom (verse 1), Nebuchadnezzar fell into a troubled sleep. When he awoke, he summoned the magicians (a better translation would be scribes or scholars), the astrologers (enchanters or conjurers), the sorcerers (those who practiced witchcraft), and the Chaldeans (priests or wise men) and asked them to tell him what he had dreamed. In response to their request to relate the dream so they could interpret it, he told them, "My decision is firm: if you do not make known the dream to me, and its interpretation, you shall be cut in pieces" (verse 5). While his reaction may sound revolting to us today, such cruelty was common in the ancient world when absolute monarchs held sway.

The King James Version, following the Septuagint (the Greek translation of the Old Testament), translates "the thing is gone from me," generally understood to mean that the king had forgotten the dream. Modern translations, following the Hebrew text, translate "my decision is firm." While the king probably said only one or the other, both statements may be true. The king, having forgotten the details of the dream, used this fact to test his counselors. If he had forgotten the dream completely, it would hardly have troubled him. Ellen White provides some insight into the situation. "The Lord in His providence had a wise purpose in view in giving Nebuchadnezzar this dream, and then causing him to forget the particulars, but to retain the fearful impression made upon his mind. The Lord desired to expose the pretensions of the wise men of Babylon."[5]

The magicians, astrologers, sorcerers, and Chaldeans had to admit that only a supernatural power could tell the king what he wanted. In so doing, they prepared the way for Daniel, who, as the story unfolds, assured the king that the God of Israel was the only one who could meet the king's challenge.

A Crisis at Daniel's House (Dan. 2:14-23)—The fact that the king did not call in Daniel and his friends indicates their junior status at the court at that time. Nevertheless, the death decree included them as well. Repeatedly throughout the book of Daniel death threatens God's people. This is of special relevance to the believers living at the end of time, for they will have to face the death threat of Revelation 13:13-18.

When Arioch, the royal executioner, stood at Daniel's door, the four young Hebrews faced a momentous crisis—extinction stared them in the face. Daniel's response to Arioch is an example of how God's children should react to any crisis. He remained calm and showed wisdom and discretion. In addition, he displayed great courage and faith. God, who had manifested His power at the beginning of their training, would not forsake them now. With God's help and his own diplomatic skills, Daniel managed to get a temporary reprieve and arrange an audience with the king. Nebuchadnezzar obviously was happy to grant a stay of execution, since he was eager to learn the meaning of the dream that Daniel promised to provide (Dan. 2:16).

Following his interview with the king, Daniel went home to hold a prayer vigil with his friends. Note how Daniel begins his prayer with "Blessed be the name of God" (verse 20). In the Old Testament people frequently blessed the Lord (Judges 5:9; Neh. 9:5; Ps. 103:1; 134:1). The Aramaic and Hebrew words for "bless" can also be translated as "praise," and this is the meaning in Daniel 2:19, 20. The heartfelt prayer of the young men for God's help received an almost immediate answer. In a night vision Daniel saw not only what Nebuchadnezzar had seen, but also what the dream meant. Before rushing off to the palace, Daniel called a meeting of praise and thanksgiving. In contrast to the fatalistic astrology of the Chaldeans, Daniel's hymn of praise emphasized that a divine mind controls history. "He removes kings and raises up kings" (verse 21).

Nebuchadnezzar's Dream (Dan. 2:24-35)—Following the praise service in his house, the prophet first showed concern for the royal counselors in Babylon. He asked Arioch to spare their lives (verse 24), a testimony to Daniel's altruistic character. In spite of just having received the information concerning Nebuchadnezzar's dream, and eager to tell the king, he was not so preoccupied with his own future that he did not think of others.

Then, as he stood before the king, he courageously told Nebuchadnezzar that no human being could find out what the king had dreamed (verse 27), but the God of heaven could reveal such secrets. The Babylonians worshiped the stars of heaven as the representatives of their gods. Daniel explained to the king that the God of the Hebrews was the Creator and ruler of the universe, and that He had revealed to him the dream and its interpretation.

The purpose of the dream, Daniel said, was to inform the king what would happen "in the latter days" (verse 28). The phrase "latter days" appears again in Daniel 10:14, in which an angel tells the prophet that he has come to make him understand what will happen to his people in the latter days. A study of this expression outside of the book of Daniel shows that the "latter days" can refer to various time periods in history. In Genesis 49:1, the first place the phrase appears, Jacob at the end of his life looks into the future and under prophetic inspiration predicts major developments in the history of his sons and their descendants. The "latter days" in this text, therefore, refer to the whole time span from the conquest of Canaan to the appearance of the Messiah.

Moses declared in Deuteronomy 31:29 that after his death the children of Israel would become utterly corrupt and that evil would befall them in "the latter days," a prophecy fulfilled in the time of the judges (Judges 2:11-16) and kings (Jer. 7:28-34), when Israel repeatedly apostatized on a large scale. Hence "the latter days" in this text refers to the period of the judges and kings. Jeremiah 23:20 and 30:24 apply "latter days" to the fall of Jerusalem in 586 B.C. Jeremiah 48:47 and 49:39 have in view the time of the Persian restoration. Other passages, notably Isaiah 2:2, Micah 4:1, and Hosea 3:5, consider the time of the messianic kingdom as "the latter days." Thus, the context must decide in each case what specific era the term intends. A better translation than "latter days" is "in the future" or "in days to come," as the RSV, NEB, and NIV have done. In Daniel 2:28 "the latter days," therefore, refers to "the future which began in the time of Daniel and reaches down to the time of the second advent of Christ, symbolized by the stone kingdom."[6]

The description of the mighty image that Nebuchadnezzar saw in his dream mentions the metals that comprise each part of the statue—the head of gold, the chest and arms of silver, the belly and thighs of bronze, and the legs of iron with the feet of iron mingled with clay—but the emphasis is on the stone, cut out of the mountain, and its effect on the statue. With incredible force it crushes and grinds the statue to dust, then fills the whole earth.

With great skill and an economy of words Daniel depicted the dream. "There is not a superfluous word in Daniel's entire description and account. It is a masterpiece of pithy word painting."[7] At no time did Daniel stop and ask, "Am I right, King Nebuchadnezzar? Is this what you saw?" His voice rang with the conviction of a man who had been in touch with God. He had heard the voice of God, and now he spoke with authority.

The Dream Interpreted (Dan. 2:36-45)—King Nebuchadnezzar must have been excited when he heard Daniel relate the dream. Now he was eager to hear its meaning. While Daniel addressed the king with the customary "king of kings," he did not seek to curry the monarch's favor. In plain language he told the king that his position on the throne had resulted, not from his own power and skill, but from the God of heaven's putting him there (verses 37, 38). Then he proceeded to interpret the dream:

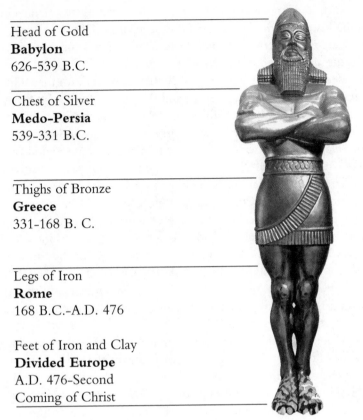

Head of Gold
Babylon
626–539 B.C.

Chest of Silver
Medo–Persia
539–331 B.C.

Thighs of Bronze
Greece
331–168 B. C.

Legs of Iron
Rome
168 B.C.–A.D. 476

Feet of Iron and Clay
Divided Europe
A.D. 476–Second
Coming of Christ

The Image of Daniel 2

1. "You are that head of gold" (verse 38). Nebuchadnezzar represented the Babylonian Empire. The book of Daniel uses kings and kingdoms interchangeably. In the days of Nebuchadnezzar Babylon was by far
the greatest and richest city in the world. Scripture, therefore, calls it the
"golden city" (Isa. 14:4, KJV; see also Jer. 51:7; Rev. 18:16).

The history of Babylon is the story of the great conflict between Christ
and Satan. The first national resistance to God recorded in Scripture came
from Babylon (Gen. 11), and in the last book of the Bible Babylon stands
as a symbol of opposition against Christ (Rev. 14:8; 16:19; 17:5). Historical
Babylon was somewhat like a counterfeit of the Garden of Eden. It too had
a great river running through it, and the ancients regarded the Hanging
Gardens of Babylon as one of the wonders of the world. At its head stood

an absolute monarch with power over life and death, though in contrast to God, the king of Babylon used his power capriciously.

Babylon, built by Nimrod (Gen. 10:10), had three periods of glory: (1) under Sargon of Akkad (2300 B.C.), when it became the first world empire in history; (2) under Hammurabi (1729-1686 B.C., famous for the Codex Hammurabi; and (3) under Nabopolassar (626-605 B.C.) and his son Nebuchadnezzar (605-562 B.C.), who made Babylon one of the most magnificent cities in the ancient world. According to Herodotus, Babylon's builders used an abundance of gold to embellish the city.

"In the temple of Babylon there is a second shrine lower down, in which is a great sitting figure of Bel, all of gold on a golden throne, supported on a base of gold, with a golden table standing beside it. I was told by the Chaldeans that, to make all this, more than twenty-two tons of gold were used. . . . In the time of Cyrus there was also in this sacred building a solid golden statue of a man some fifteen feet high—I have this on the authority of the Chaldeans, though I never saw it myself."[8]

2. "Another kingdom inferior to yours . . ." (Dan. 2:39). Medo-Persia and Greece receive only brief treatments. Daniel is chiefly concerned with the first and the last empires. Medo-Persia (539-331 B.C.) was not inferior in size or in the length of its existence, but it was distinctly inferior to Babylon in luxury, magnificence, and complexity of civilization. The reference to silver alludes to the fact that the Persians used silver in their taxation system. Each satrapy paid its tribute in silver talents, except that of the Indian satrapy, the richest of all, which paid in gold.[9]

3. "A third kingdom of bronze" (verse 39). The third kingdom was Greece (331-168 B.C.). Alexander the Great conquered Medo-Persia (336-323 B.C.). The Greeks commonly employed bronze in trade (Eze. 27:13) and warfare. Greek soldiers were noted for their bronze armor. Their helmets, shields, and battle-axes consisted of brass. Herodotus tells us that Psammetichus I of Egypt saw in invading Greek pirates the fulfillment of an oracle that foretold "men of bronze coming from the sea."[10]

4. "The fourth kingdom shall be as strong as iron" (Dan. 2:40). The fourth kingdom was the Roman Empire (168 B.C.-A.D. 476). As artisans can use an iron hammer to work gold, silver, and bronze, so, prophecy predicted, the fourth kingdom would be stronger than all its predecessors. From history we know that the iron legions of Rome crushed and demolished all resistance. Rome conquered all the Hellenistic kingdoms. The first to fall was Macedonia in 168 B.C. In that year the Roman general Paulus defeated Perseus, the king of Macedon, at Pydna, and when in 30

B.C. Cleopatra, the queen of Egypt, committed suicide, the last of the Hellenistic kingdoms became a Roman province. Rome ruled more territory than all the kingdoms before it. And whereas the previous three empires had each ruled about 200 years or less, the Roman Empire lasted for more than 600 years. It defeated one part of the ancient world after another and set up a system of government in all its provinces that became a model for the European states for centuries afterward.

5. "The feet and toes, partly of potter's clay and partly of iron" (verse 41). The last part of the statue receives the most attention (verses 41-43). The symbolism in these verses suggests that the iron empire of Rome would experience a partition and deterioration, but that a weakened and changed form of the fourth empire would continue and bridge the gap between the fourth kingdom and the universal stone kingdom. In history we see how various forces divided, carved up, and transformed the mighty Roman Empire during a number of centuries. From the strongest and most unified political unit in the world, Rome became the weakest and most divided. By A.D. 476 Odoacer, leader of the German mercenaries in the service of Rome, had deposed the last Roman emperor, Romulus Augustulus. In the years that followed, Germanic tribes who descended upon the Roman Empire from the north carved up the western area of the Roman Empire. Though the eastern Roman Empire continued for several centuries, in time it too was conquered and partitioned. And out of the ruins of the once-mighty empire arose many of the nations of Europe, some strong, some weak, stretching from the Black Sea to the Atlantic.

The text tells us that attempts to unite the various nations "with the seed of men" will arise, yet they will not hold together (verse 43). The mingling with the seed of men alludes to intermarriage between the different ruling houses of Europe. Among the various houses of royalty, the Hapsburgs were known for their motto: *"Bella gerant alii, tu felix Austria nube* [others may go to war; you, happy Austria, marry]." They acquired much territory through political marriages.

At the beginning of the past century the royal houses of Europe, through intermarriage, were all closely related with each other. George H. Merritt in 1914 wrote that "Europe at war can almost be likened to a huge family quarrel. The royal houses, especially the countries which are most vitally concerned by the war, are practically all of the same Germanic stock, and almost of one blood. There have been so many intermarriages between these houses that German blood dominates every

European throne with the exception of the two small kingdoms of Serbia and Montenegro." [11]

In spite of intermarriages and political treaties, however, nothing has successfully and permanently united Europe again since the days of the Roman Empire, though many have attempted it, e.g., Charlemagne, Charles V of Spain, Napoleon, and Hitler. All of them have failed. Will the European Common Market and the single currency concept negate this picture? No! Even though these nations may enter into agreements to facilitate trade and commerce, yet each of them will remain a separate cultural, linguistic, and territorial entity. Inspiration tells us that "we need not, and cannot, expect union among the nations of the earth. Our position in the image of Nebuchadnezzar is represented by the toes, in a divided state, and of a crumbling material, that will not hold together." [12]

The final element in Nebuchadnezzar's vision was the stone "cut out . . . without hands" (verse 45). According to Scripture, the stone represents Jesus Christ (1 Cor. 10:4; Isa. 28:16; Luke 20:17, 18), and the fact that it hit the feet and toes of the image, and not its head, body, or legs, indicates that the smiting represents Jesus' second advent at the end of time. "In the days of these kings" (Dan. 2:44) refers to the many European nations that arose out of the Roman Empire and that still exist today. The fifth kingdom of the vision is earth's last kingdom: it "shall never be destroyed; . . . it shall stand forever" (verse 44).

The King's Response (Dan. 2:46-49)—By the end of his explanations Daniel had convinced the king that his dream had indeed come from a supernatural source. He acknowledged Daniel's God as the ruler of the universe. Furthermore, the king saw his own place in world history, and he understood that his authority was under the control of the God who had given it to him (verses 37, 47).

The text tells us that the king made Daniel a prominent man (verse 48). Yet at his moment of triumph Daniel did not forget those who had joined in prayer with him. As soon as his position was decided, he requested the king to appoint his three friends to administer the affairs of the province of which Nebuchadnezzar had made Daniel ruler. On the surface this request seems simple enough, but we must remember that most likely native Babylonians had to give up their positions to make room for these unknown Jews. In God's providence the participants in Daniel's prayer now shared in his promotion. Unlike the chief butler in the story of Joseph (Gen. 40:23), Daniel did not forget his friends.

Application

While Daniel 2 teaches us much about God's role in world history, it also contains many spiritual lessons for today:

1. The Power of United Prayer—When Daniel returned home from his visit to the king's palace, where he had received a temporary reprieve, he invited his friends to join him in prayer. Many hands are better, not only when work needs to be done, but also in prayer. "If two of you agree on earth concerning anything that they ask," Jesus says, "it will be done for them by My Father in heaven" (Matt. 18:19). "Christ here shows that there must be union with others, even in our desires for a given object. Great importance is attached to the united prayer, the union of purpose."[13] Throughout Scripture we discover the truth of these words. Esther asked her servants and all the Jews in Shushan to fast and pray with her before she went in to see the king (Esther 4:16). Jesus requested His disciples to watch and pray with Him in the Garden of Gethsemane (Matt. 26:41). Prior to the outpouring of the Holy Spirit the disciples were united in prayer (Acts 1:14), and Peter's deliverance from prison took place in answer to the united prayer of the early church (Acts 12:5).

2. The Power of Earnest Prayer—The young Hebrews' prayer involved issues of life and death as they offered it in faith (James 1:6), in submission to God's will, and from the right motive. They prayed that God might spare human life and that His name be glorified. And God heard and answered their prayer, because "the effective, fervent prayer of a righteous man avails much" (James 5:16).

3. The Blessings of Prayer—The prayer of the four young Hebrews saved not only their own lives, but also those of the magicians, astrologers, sorcerers, and Chaldeans in Babylon. And it brought peace of mind to the troubled king. The prayers and the presence of godly people have often brought great blessings to others, even unbelievers. For example, the Lord blessed Potiphar's household because of the presence of Joseph in its midst (Gen. 39:5), and when a fierce storm shipwrecked a Roman vessel on the coast of Malta, not a person perished, because the apostle Paul was on board (Acts 27:24).

4. The Value of Prophecy—Daniel 2 is one of the greatest prophecies of the Bible. Apart from foretelling the future, prophecy seeks to edify and comfort believers (1 Cor. 14:3). Divine prophecy demonstrates that our world is a ship under control, rather than a drifting iceberg. It assures us that we are not alone in a senseless universe, and that a God in heaven provides for every person. Daniel 2 also teaches that everything and everyone on this earth will eventually perish unless linked to God. We are all on our way to eternal nothingness unless we take hold of the hand of God.

[1] E. J. Young, *The Prophecy of Daniel* (Grand Rapids: Eerdmans Pub., 1977), p. 56.

[2] *The Seventh-day Adventist Bible Dictionary* (Washington, D.C.: Review and Herald Pub. Assn., 1979), p. 198.

[3] Joyce G. Baldwin, *Daniel,* Tyndale Old Testament Commentary (Downers Grove, Ill.: InterVarsity Press, 1978), p. 97.

[4] Gerhard F. Hasel, "The Four World Empires of Daniel 2 Against Its Near Eastern Environment," *Journal for the Study of the Old Testament* 12 (1979): 20. We have a similar situation in the case of the Mosaic laws. God adapted many of them from already-existing laws in Mesopotamia, e.g., from Hammurabi's law code. See I. M. Price, O. R. Sellers, and E. L. Carlson, *The Monuments and the Old Testament* (Chicago: Judson Press, 1958), pp. 187-195.

[5] Ellen G. White, in *Youth's Instructor,* Sept. 1, 1903.

[6] Gerhard Pfandl, "Daniel's 'Time of the End,'" *Journal of the Adventist Theological Society* 7, no. 1 (1996): 151.

[7] H. C. Leupold, *Exposition of Daniel* (Grand Rapids: Baker Book House, 1949), pp. 110, 111.

[8] Herodotus 1. 183, in *Loeb Classical Library,* vol. 1, p. 227.

[9] Herodotus 3. 94, in *Loeb Classical Library,* vol. 2, p. 123.

[10] Herodotus 2. 152, in *Loeb Classical Library,* vol. 1, pp. 463-465.

[11] George H. Merritt, "The Royal Relatives of Europe," in *The World's Work,* May-October 1914, p. 594.

[12] Ellen G. White, *Testimonies for the Church* (Mountain View, Calif.: Pacific Press Pub. Assn., 1948), vol. 1, p. 361.

[13] *Ibid.,* vol. 3, p. 429.

CHAPTER 3

The Fiery Furnace

The story of the confrontation between the three Hebrew captives and King Nebuchadnezzar reminds us of the battle between David and Goliath. In both cases the odds were heavily in favor of the pagans. The struggle pitted human power against faith, and faith seemed to have drawn the short straw, but in both cases it triumphed. The secret of the safety of the three Hebrews in the fiery furnace was the presence of Immanuel (God with us) in their midst. He went with them into the blazing furnace, not only to honor their faith, but to demonstrate to the assembled leaders of the Babylonian Empire the might of the power of the God of Jerusalem.

Information

Ancient Statues—It was a common practice in the ancient Near East for kings to set up statues of themselves with flattering inscriptions in their provinces and conquered territories as a symbol of their dominion. Museums display huge Egyptian and Assyrian statues. Ancient reports indicate that many others existed. The Greek historian Diodorus (first century B.C.) mentions a figure of Zeus 40 feet high, and the colossus at Rhodes at 105 feet (70 cubits) was higher than Nebuchadnezzar's statue.[1]

The Plain of Dura—The term *dur* means "wall" or "fortress," the letter *a* at the end being the Aramaic article. Interpreters have favored one of two sites for the plain of Dura. The first is located about six miles south of ancient Babylon, where a series of mounds still bear the Arabic name Tulul Dura (mounds of Dura). Archaeologists uncovered there a platform about 20 feet high and 45 feet square that could have served as a base for the image.

The second site is thought to have been between the two major walls surrounding the city of Babylon. Excavations have revealed that the inner city, which Nebuchadnezzar inherited, was almost square, with walls about one mile long on each side. It contained palaces, administrative buildings, the temple complex called Esaglia, as well as many other dwellings. Nebuchadnezzar built a new palace to the north of the city on the bank of the river Euphrates and added a large outer wall several miles in extent to enclose the expanded city and his new summer palace. "In Nebuchadnezzar's time, Babylonian engineers and builders had not yet filled this area between the inner and outer walls with buildings, although construction was taking place. The open area served as parade ground for the army and a place within the city walls where troops could bivouac. This large open space between the two walls could properly be called the 'plain of the wall,' or 'plain of Dura.' In all likelihood this was where the events of chapter 3 took place."[2]

The Date of the Golden Image—The Hebrew Bible gives no date for the events in Daniel 3. The Greek (Septuagint) and the Syriac (Peshitta) versions of the Old Testament add at the beginning of verse 1 "In the eighteenth year of Nebuchadnezzar," which would be 587 B.C., one year before the fall of Jerusalem. This date, however, is too late, since the siege of the city that preceded its capture lasted for more than one year (2 Kings 25:1-8).

A more likely date could have been the revolt in 595/594 in which, according to the Babylonian Chronicle, the king "slew many of his own army."[3] The dedication of the image would allow all the king's officials to show their allegiance to him publicly. It was Nebuchadnezzar's way of solidifying control over the various elements of his vast empire.

According to Jeremiah 51:59 Zedekiah in his fourth year made a journey to Babylon, possibly in response to Nebuchadnezzar's summons mentioned in Daniel 3:2.

Explanation

Nebuchadnezzar's Image of Gold (Dan. 3:1-7)—The period of Nebuchadnezzar's rule was a golden age for Babylon. His reign constituted the pinnacle of Babylonian power and glory. In his remarkable dream in chapter 2 he had seen his empire as the golden head of the image. Here in this chapter we find him making an entire image from gold. The Greek historian Herodotus (fifth century B.C.) reports that in the days of Cyrus local informants told him that "there was still in this sacred demesne a statue of solid gold twelve cubits [18 feet] high."[4] Nebuchadnezzar's image, however, was 60 cubits (90 feet) high and six cubits (9 feet) wide (Dan. 3:1). Most likely it consisted of wood covered with gold leaf. The

Babylon

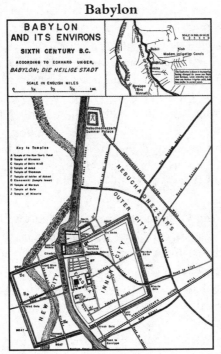

Source: F. D. Nichol, ed., *The Seventh-day Adventist Bible Commentary* (Washington, D.C.: Review and Herald Pub. Assn., 1955), vol. 4, p. 796.

proportions given in the text would yield a rather grotesque figure, too thin for its height. Many interpreters therefore assume that the 60 cubits included a high base or pedestal.

Why did Nebuchadnezzar erect this image? For a time after the vision in Daniel 2, it seems, the fear of God continued to influence him. However, "the prosperity attending his reign filled him with pride," and in time he "resumed his idol worship with increased zeal and bigotry."[5] The golden image most likely reflected the dream-image that Nebuchadnezzar had seen, but he determined that his image should be entirely of gold—a symbol of the kingdom of Babylon that should stand forever.

The Charge Against the Young Hebrews (Dan. 3:8-12)—When the music sounded and everybody fell down to worship the golden image, the three young Hebrews, who refused to bow, stood out like a sore thumb. "Fall down and worship the golden image," Nebuchadnezzar had ordered. But "you shall not bow down and worship any carved image" their God had commanded (see Ex. 20:4, 5). Probably some of those next to them urged them to comply. "Didn't you hear the music? Get down or you're dead." But Shadrach, Meshach, and Abednego remained standing, three lonely figures in a sea of idol worshipers. Daniel must have been elsewhere, or he would have stood with his friends. The ceremony of dedication represented an act of worship to the power and might of Nebuchadnezzar, and this the three Hebrews refused to do. We note here the close connection between the state and its religion. This kind of union has in fact characterized most nations throughout history. The separation of church and state as we know it today is a fairly recent phenomenon.

The Confrontation (Dan. 3:13-18)—In so vast a crowd the king probably could not see that three men were still standing, so certain Chaldeans took it upon themselves to inform him. The men were jealous of the honors bestowed on Daniel's friends (see Dan. 2), and they gladly took the opportunity to report them to the king. Forgetting that they owed their lives to the young men, they blamed the king for placing the captives in such high positions and thereby inviting defiance.

When the king's soldiers brought Shadrach, Meshach, and Abednego before him, he was amazed. "Is it true?" he asked (Dan. 3:14). Apparently he found it difficult to believe that three of the top administrators in his empire would refuse to obey his command. Still he was anxious to save them, though he had to do it in a way that defended his honor. So he offered them another chance: "Now if you are ready . . ." However, should they continue to disobey, the fiery furnace would be their fate. To make sure they understood he meant it, he added a challenge to their God. "And who is the God who will deliver you from my hands?" Nebuchadnezzar knew from experience that there was a God who could reveal secrets (Dan. 2), but it appears that he did not believe that this Deity could also save the Hebrews from the burning furnace.

The answer of the three captives has gone down in history. "Don't trouble yourself with another trial," they said in effect; "we will not bow down, even if our God does not deliver us." They didn't doubt that God could rescue them if it served His purpose, but the question was Would He? Still, they had made up their minds. Even if God did not step in, they would not compromise their faith, but would remain obedient to the Word of God. How easy it would have been for them to rationalize. "If we bow down, we will live and will continue to occupy positions in the government, which means we will be able to help our people when they need it." Or: "We can bow down and pray to God to forgive us."

However, nothing in the text indicates that the young Hebrews entertained such thoughts. Instead they stood their ground. Their attitude has inspired God's people ever since.

At the time of the Korean War Communist forces invaded a Korean village. There they found a young man who, regardless of their edicts to the contrary, continued to witness for Christ. Determined to make a public example of him, the Communists commanded the entire village to appear in the town square. One of the officers led the young Christian in front of the crowd, put a pistol to his head, and shouted, "Denounce Jesus Christ or die!" When the young man saw some of those he had led to Christ in the crowd, he raised his head and cried, "I believe in Jesus Christ; I believe . . ." *Crack!* The pistol shot ended his life. He and many others like him reflected the courage and faith of Shadrach, Meshach, and Abednego.[6]

Saved in Fiery Trial (Dan. 3:19-25)—The speech of the young men infuriated the king. He ordered his "mighty men" to heat the furnace "seven times more," i.e., to heat it to the fullest extent, and then throw the three Hebrews into the flames.

The fiery furnace was probably a brick kiln fed by straw saturated with crude oil. "The city of Babylon was made of thousands, if not millions, of clay bricks. The kilns used to fire these bricks were shaped like a beehive with a hole at the top of the cone through which flammable material was dropped; there was another tunnel-like opening on one side. Pallets of bricks were put in the side opening, and the material with which the kiln was fired was dropped into the kiln from above. Steps went up the side of the kiln to the upper opening. The Hebrews were probably dropped into the kiln through the hole at the top."[7]

The furnace was so hot that the blast of heat killed the soldiers who threw them in; but when the king looked through the opening on the side, instead of seeing the three Hebrews consumed by the flames he noticed them walking in the midst of the fire. God literally fulfilled for them the promise found in Isaiah 43:2: "When you walk through the fire, you shall not be burned, nor shall the flame scorch you." But more than that, not only did Nebuchadnezzar observe the three Hebrews walking about freely in the furnace; he saw a fourth figure with them who resembled the "Son of God" (Dan. 3:25). "The same Christ who appeared to Adam in Eden, who walked with Enoch and talked with Noah, who wrestled with Jacob and feasted with Abraham, who appeared to Moses in the burning bush and to Joshua on the walls of Jericho, again stepped from the heavenly portals and entered the fiery furnace to succor and support His faithful followers. The form of the fourth is always in the midst of His holy people."[8]

The King Worships God (Dan. 3:26-30)—Staring into the flames, the king could hardly believe his eyes. Admitting defeat, he addressed Shadrach, Meshach, and Abednego as "servants of the Most High God" and asked them to come out. The service of dedication halted, and everyone ignored the image while the king publicly confessed his mistake. He acknowledged that the God of the Hebrews had delivered the young men, and he commended them on their trust in God (verse 28).

The chapter that began with a decree threatening the lives of the three Hebrews because of their loyalty to the God of heaven now closes with a second decree aimed at anyone who speaks a word against the God of the Hebrews. While it was right for the king to make public confession and to seek to exalt the God of heaven above all other gods, "in endeavoring to force his subjects to make a similar confession of faith and to show similar reverence, Nebuchadnezzar was exceeding his right as a temporal sovereign. He had no more right, either civil or moral, to threaten men with death for not worshiping God, than he had to make the decree consigning to the flames all who refused to worship the golden image. God never compels the obedience of man. He leaves all free to choose whom they will serve."[9]

Application

The event on the plain of Dura is the first recorded instance of a government attempting to achieve conformity through worship. King Nebuchadnezzar attempted to enforce uniformity of worship by attaching a death decree to the ceremony of the golden image. According to prophecy, God's people in the time of the end will face a similar decree through modern Babylon.

A comparison between Daniel 3 and Revelation 13:11-18 indicates that (1) the issue is worship in both chapters; (2) both chapters have an image to worship, one literal, the other a spiritual one; (3) in Daniel 3 literal Babylon demanded this worship, while in Revelation 13 spiritual Babylon will require the worship of the image to the beast; (4) the three Hebrews faced death. In the future, church and state will unite to enforce uniformity of worship. Those who refuse to submit will face economic boycott and, ultimately, also the death penalty (Rev. 13:15).

This chapter offers several lessons for us:

1. In the great controversy between Christ and Satan the believer is always on the winning side (Rom. 8:28).

37

2. Throughout history God's children have always received help in times of need (Heb. 4:16). The three Hebrews "were already committed to the flames before they knew precisely what form that grace would take. Would it be the grace of deliverance or the grace to die well for God's glory? Only in the moment of trial did it become clear exactly how God would show His faithfulness."[10] And so it is with us today (Ps. 66:10-12).

3. The issue of idolatry is not confined to the past. Anything that replaces God in the lives of His people today can become an idol. The human mind, John Calvin said, is a "factory of idols." Pleasure seeking, the acquisition of knowledge, or material wealth can today become idols. The essence of modern idolatry is the idol of self. To avoid bowing to this idol in any of its manifestations we must direct our worship to Jesus, who alone is "the image of the invisible God" (Col. 1:15).

4. The final lesson we can take away from the incident is the whole-hearted commitment of the three Hebrews. "There is no limit to the usefulness of one who, putting self aside, makes room for the working of the Holy Spirit upon his heart and lives a life wholly consecrated to God."[11]

[1] James Montgomery, *The Book of Daniel,* International Critical Commentary (Edinburgh: T. and T. Clark, 1979), pp. 193, 194.

[2] William H. Shea, *Daniel 1-7,* Abundant Life Bible Amplifier (Boise, Idaho: Pacific Press Pub. Assn., 1996), p. 104.

[3] D. J. Wiseman, *Chronicles of Chaldean Kings* (London: Trustees of the British Museum, 1956), p. 73.

[4] Herodotus 1. 183, in *Loeb Classical Library,* vol. 1, p. 229.

[5] E. G. White, *Prophets and Kings,* p. 504.

[6] Adapted from Donald K. Campbell, *Daniel: Decoder of Dreams* (Wheaton, Ill.: Victor Books, 1977), pp. 31, 32.

[7] Shea, p. 110.

[8] W. G. Heslop, *Diamonds From Daniel* (Nazarene Publishing House, 1937), pp. 64, 65.

[9] White, *Prophets and Kings,* pp. 510, 511.

[10] Sinclair Ferguson, *Daniel,* Mastering the Old Testament (Dallas: Word Publishing, 1988), p. 86.

[11] Ellen G. White, *The Ministry of Healing* (Mountain View, Calif.: Pacific Press Pub. Assn., 1942), p. 159.

38

CHAPTER 4

Nebuchadnezzar's Judgment

Daniel 4 contains one of the most remarkable stories in the Bible. It is a public testimony by one of the greatest kings of ancient times, telling of his pride, humiliation, and ultimate conversion to the Ruler of heaven. Nebuchadnezzar's life prior to this event had been one long success story. By military might he had subdued all the surrounding nations. "At his feet bowed the representatives of all nations and into his coffers flowed the wealth from every quarter. He was surrounded by the wit and learning of the times, and under his patronage the arts flourished."[1] But at the height of his power God brought him low. It is a story of warning to us all, that if we make our happiness depend on anything less than heaven, we invite destruction.

Information

Nebuchadnezzar, the Royal Builder—Babylon, excavated between 1899 and 1917 by R. Koldewey, covered an area of about two square miles. A system of double walls about 10 miles long and up to 26 feet wide surrounded the city. It was a religious center without rival. "A cuneiform tablet of Nebuchadnezzar's time lists 53 temples dedicated to important gods, 955 small sanctuaries, and 384 street altars—all of them within the city confines."[2] In an inscription from Babylon Nebuchadnezzar claims: "I have made Babylon, the holy city, the glory of the great gods, more prominent than before, and have promoted its rebuilding. I have caused the sanctuaries of gods and goddesses to lighten up like the day. No king among all kings has ever created, no earlier king has ever built, what I have magnificently built for Marduk."[3]

The center of Babylon's glory was the famous temple tower Etemenanki, dedicated to the god Marduk. Three hundred feet square at the base, it stood more than 300 feet high. In ancient times only the two great pyramids at Gizah in Egypt surpassed it in size.

During his 43-year reign Nebuchadnezzar built three palaces. The Southern Palace contained, among other structures, the famous Hanging Gardens of Babylon, something like roof gardens or garden terraces and considered one of the seven wonders of the ancient world. It was built for the king's Median wife as a substitute for the wooded hills of her native land. Another of the city's colorful structures was the famous Ishtar Gate, through which passed the Procession Street, leading from the various palaces to the temple Esagila.

Tree Symbolism in the Ancient Near East—Sacred or cosmic trees were a major element of the iconography of ancient Mesopotamia. Many seals from the Neo-Assyrian and Neo-Babylonian time (1000-500 B.C.) de-

pict such trees. Usually in the center of the image is a sacred palm tree. Above the tree is a winged sun disk with a feathered tail, representing the sun god. From the wings two streams of water flow down along the sides of the sacred tree. On either side of the tree appear representations of kings or priests in the act of worship. The

Source: Martin Klingbeil, *Yahweh Fighting From Heaven* (Goettingen: Vandenhoeck and Ruprecht, 1999), p. 213.

tree, says S. Parpola, "represents the divine world order maintained by the king as the representative of the god Assur, embodied in the winged disk hovering above the Tree."[4] Sometimes the king takes the place of the tree, and "in such scenes the king is portrayed as the human personification of the Tree. Thus if the Tree symbolized the divine world order, then the king himself represented the realization of that order in man, in other words, a true image of God, the Perfect Man."[5]

Nebuchadnezzar's Sickness—In 1952 archaeologists discovered an Aramaic fragment of a prayer of thanksgiving attributed to Nabonidus, the last king of Babylon, in Qumran Cave 4. The text mentions that the king had an unpleasant skin disease by the ordinance of God Most High for seven years. When scholars first published the fragment, many assumed that it was an early version of the story in Daniel 4, and that the book of Daniel substituted the name of Nebuchadnezzar for Nabonidus. Conservative scholars, however, believe that this fragment may possibly be "a late, garbled tradition of the illness of Nebuchadnezzar himself, if indeed it does not represent a later illness that actually befell Nabonidus personally (whose 10 years of confinement to the North Arabian city of Teima [Teman] may have been partly occasioned by illness)."[6]

Explanation

Nebuchadnezzar's Hymn of Praise (Dan. 4:1-3)—The chapter opens with a proclamation to all his subjects. The customary greeting "Peace be multiplied to you" (verse 1; cf. Gen. 43:23; Luke 10:5) is the salutation that people use when they meet each other even today in the Middle East—Shalom, or Salam. Yet in this case it comes from a man who has truly found peace himself. The once-proud monarch was at peace with himself and the world, and he wanted everyone to know why. Humbly he explains the purpose of this testimony: "I thought it good to declare the signs and wonders that the Most High God has worked for me" (Dan. 4:2).

The signs and wonders Nebuchadnezzar is referring to were the manifestations of God's power in his life. God communicated to him indirectly in chapter 1 through the four young Hebrews who were 10 times brighter than all the others. Then He addressed him directly in chapter 2 through the dream of the great image, and He more than spoke to him from the fiery furnace in chapter 3. Although He knocked hard at the door of the king's heart, the king was not yet ready for God to enter. In chapter 4 the Lord once more tries to get through to Nebuchadnezzar, and this time He knocks so hard that the door comes right off its hinges. But eventually God does enter Nebuchadnezzar's heart. God's patience and long-suffering demonstrate that He is in no hurry to punish but waits patiently for each prodigal to return home.

The Search for an Interpreter (Dan. 4:4-18)—Toward the end of his life Nebuchadnezzar recounts the most dramatic events in his life: his insanity and the subsequent recovery, which culminated in his acceptance of God's rulership in his life. He begins by stating that he was both "at rest" and "flourishing" (verse 4). In other words, he was prosperous and content with himself, like the man in the parable of the rich fool (Luke 12:16-21). In the twenty-first century we could compare him to a wealthy landowner who has just checked with his stockbroker and discovered that he indeed has reason to be contented.

41

God, however, had a different view. He gave Nebuchadnezzar a dream that troubled him (Dan. 4:5). As he had done previously, he immediately issued an order for the counselors of the realm to appear before him. But in contrast to the story in chapter 2, on this occasion he told them the dream. Once again they are unable to explain to the king its meaning—or perhaps because of the dream's negative content they preferred to remain silent rather than risk the ruler's ire.

When at last Daniel, in response to the royal summons, stood before Nebuchadnezzar, the king acknowledged that "the Spirit of the Holy God" was in the prophet (verse 9), and therefore he would surely be able to explain the meaning of the dream. The delay in Daniel's appearance, the cause of which is unknown, serves to emphasize the difference between the court officials, who used traditional dream interpretation techniques, and Daniel, who had received the gift of interpretation from God.

At the center of the king's dream is a great tree that reaches up to the heavens, providing food and shelter for all living creatures. Trees play an important part in Scripture. In Genesis 3 we find the tree of life in the midst of the Garden of Eden. Psalm 1 compares God's people to trees planted by rivers, and Ezekiel 31 describes Assyria as a cedar of Lebanon. Jesus frequently used trees to illustrate important truths (Matt. 7:17, 18; 12:33; 24:32, 33), and Paul compared faithful Israel to an olive tree and the Gentiles to grafted-in branches (Rom. 11:17).

The tree in Daniel 4 is a symbol of King Nebuchadnezzar himself. In his dream he saw a being, a watcher, a holy one, descending from heaven and ordering the tree cut down (verse 14). The veil that hides the unseen world lifted for a moment, as it does elsewhere in Daniel, and humanity caught a glimpse behind the curtain where the cosmic struggle between Christ and Satan rages. Patterned on the book of Daniel, such unseen watchers appeared frequently in Jewish literature of the Hellenistic and Roman period.[7]

The stump that Nebuchadnezzar sees remaining seems to indicate that although the king is to be removed from power, he is not to be destroyed completely. Some evidence from ancient Mesopotamian exists for the use of metal bands on trees, whether to prevent them from cracking or for some other reason that is not clear. Such bronze rings were unearthed in Khorsabad. Bands of metal also appear around the trunk of a tree on cylinder seals and slabs from the palace of Ashurnasirpal (885–860 B.C.) at Nimrud.[8]

The Dream Interpreted (Dan. 4:19-27)—Daniel was distressed, even stunned, by the severity of the divine judgment against the king. He hesitated to give the interpretation, not because he was worried what might happen to him as the bearer of bad news, but rather because he felt concerned for the well-being of the king. But the meaning of the dream was clear without much interpretation, so Daniel came right to the point: "You, O king, are symbolized by the tree." Most likely Nebuchadnezzar already suspected it to be the case. In an inscription at the Wady Brissa he compared his empire to a great tree: "Under its everlasting shadow [that is, of Babylon], I have gathered all the peoples in peace."[9]

Since Nebuchadnezzar is the tree, he is also the subject of the coming judgment. "They shall drive you from men, your dwelling shall be with the beasts of the field, and they shall make you eat grass like oxen" (verse 25). For what purpose? The answer provides the theological focus of this chapter: "till you know that the Most High rules in the kingdom of men, and gives it to whomever he chooses." Already in chapter 2 events had brought this message home to the king, but he had refused to accept it. God, therefore, would deal severely with him to cure him of his spiritual blindness. He would lose his royal glory and be reduced to the level of a brute beast. "According to the dream, 'the beasts of the field [had] found shade' under Nebuchadnezzar, the cosmic tree (v. 12); now God would reduce him to being one of those beasts who needed shelter and provision."[10]

Daniel ventured a twofold word of advice in the hope of averting the dreadful sentence pronounced upon the king: 1. "Break off your sins by being righteous" (Dan. 4:27), i.e., "repent and do what is right." Repentance is a constant theme throughout Scripture. The first recorded word of John the Baptist was "Repent" (Matt. 3:2); and the first recorded word of Jesus as an adult on earth also was "Repent" (Matt. 4:17). There is no such thing as salvation apart from repentance. 2. Show "mercy to the poor" (Dan. 4:27). Both the Old and New Testaments voice this concern. Those who have no influence and none to plead their cause suffer much abuse.

The Fulfillment of the Dream (Dan. 4:28-33)—The last verses of the chapter report the details of the tragedy: "All this came upon King Nebuchadnezzar" (verse 28). Yet God graciously delayed the judgment for 12 months to give Nebuchadnezzar time to respond to Daniel's counsel. Following a boastful speech by Nebuchadnezzar, however, a voice from heaven announced the fulfillment of the divine judgment (verse 33).

The sickness of Nebuchadnezzar has been the subject of considerable debate. He suffered possibly from a form of insanity, in which human beings think that they are animals. It could have been lycanthropy, the wolf-man syndrome, or boanthropy, in which a person thinks he or she is an ox. A Babylonian cuneiform text, published in 1975, may refer to Nebuchadnezzar's madness. The text states that the king "gave contradictory orders, refused to accept the counsel of his courtiers, showed love neither to his son nor daughter, neglected his family, and no longer performed his duties as head of state."[11] Because of his mental illness his officials most likely confined him to the precincts of the royal palace, rather than let him be exposed to the gaze of the multitudes, and his ministers and counselors handled the affairs of state. But God protected the king from the kind of revolts that often sprang up during periods of royal weakness.

Concluding Doxology (Dan. 4:34-37)—The story concludes with the restoration of Nebuchadnezzar to the throne of Babylon. Realizing what had happened to him, he used his restored reason to bless, praise, and honor God. Was Nebuchadnezzar truly converted? It seems so. Ellen White wrote that "the once proud monarch had become a humble child of God; the tyrannical, overbearing ruler, a wise and compassionate king. He who had defied and blasphemed the God of heaven now acknowledged the power of the Most High and earnestly sought to promote the fear of Jehovah and the happiness of his subjects."[12]

Application

Daniel 4 contains many lessons: 1. The principle that Nebuchadnezzar took a long time to learn is still valid today—that God is in control of the universe and has assigned to each individual a place and a task in His great plan. 2. Humanity may avert God's judgments by repentance and conversion (see Isa. 38:1, 2, 5; Jer. 18:7-10; Jonah 3:1-10). For this reason God announced the impending judgment upon Nebuchadnezzar but gave him a full year in which to repent and thus avoid the threatened calamity (see Dan. 4:29). 3. We should never despair about the conversion of anybody. Who would have thought that this pagan king would one day be among God's great witnesses to the world? 4. Daniel 4 graphically reveals the danger of pride. Nebuchadnezzar may be an extreme example, but pride to a greater or lesser degree resides in all human beings, and it comes in endless forms. It is vital therefore to remember the inspired counsel: "A man's pride will bring him low, but the humble in spirit will retain honor" (Prov. 29:23). 5. As with most of the chapters in Daniel, this one also has special significance for "the time of the end." Revelation 18:7 tells us that the latter-day Babylon, the final church-state confederacy, will boast, "I sit as queen, and am no widow, and will not see sorrow," but, as with Nebuchadnezzar, such bragging is only the prelude to judgment and destruction.

[1] Desmond Ford, "The Centuries in a Nutshell," *Ministry,* May 1974, p. 21.

[2] *The Seventh-day Adventist Bible Commentary* (Washington, D.C.: Review and Herald Pub. Assn., 1955), vol. 4, p. 797.

[3] *Ibid.,* p. 799.

[4] S. Parpola, "The Assyrian Tree of Life: Tracing the Origins of the Jewish Monotheism and Greek Philosophy," *Journal of Near Eastern Studies* 52 (1993): 167. See also Martin Klingbeil, *Yahweh Fighting From Heaven* (Goettingen: Vandenhoeck and Ruprecht, 1999), p. 213.

[5] Parpola, pp. 167, 168.

[6] Gleason L. Archer, "Daniel," *The Expositor's Bible Commentary* (Grand Rapids: Zondervan, 1985), vol. 7, p. 63.

[7] For example, in 1 Enoch 1-36 we find the "Book of Watchers," in which the term refers to fallen angels, e.g., 1 Enoch 14:1, 3. See James H. Charlesworth, ed., *The Old Testament Pseudepigrapha* (Garden City, N.Y.: Doubleday and Company, Inc., 1983), vol. 1, p. 20.

[8] See John J. Collins, *Daniel,* Hermeneia (Minneapolis: Fortress Press, 1993), p. 226.

[9] Stephen Langdon, ed., *Building Inscriptions of the Neo-Babylonian Empire: Nabopolassar and Nebuchadnezzar* (Paris: E. Leroux, 1905), p. 171, in Donald E. Gowan, *Daniel,* Abingdon Old Testament Commentaries (Nashville: Abingdon Press, 2001), p. 80.

[10] S. Ferguson, *Daniel,* p. 97.

[11] Siegfried H. Horn, "New Light on Nebuchadnezzar's Madness," *Ministry,* April 1978, p. 40.

[12] E. G. White, *Prophets and Kings,* p. 521.

Surprise Party

In 1976 Americans celebrated the 200th anniversary of their nation's birth. Anyone who visits Washington, D.C., today can study the original copies of the Declaration of Independence, the Constitution, and the Bill of Rights. The creators of such documents were individuals of great foresight, yet they could hardly have envisaged that one day America would be the world's leading superpower. But nations not only rise—they also fall. Daniel 5 records the collapse of a great nation—Babylon. In chapter 2 Daniel had told Nebuchadnezzar that three other world powers would succeed his kingdom. Chapter 5 records the fulfillment of the first part of this prophecy as Persia replaced Babylon.

Information

King Belshazzar—Until the year 1861 Bible critics stumbled over the first words of the chapter, "Belshazzar the king," because the ancient sources available at that time reported that Nabonidus was the last ruler of Babylon. The name Belshazzar did not appear in any ancient document. Therefore, they claimed, Belshazzar was an invention of the biblical author. In 1861, however, excavators found the first cuneiform tablet with Belshazzar's name on it. Epigraphists in 1882 translated the Nabonidus Chronicle, which states that Nabonidus lived in Tema (about 500 miles south of Babylon) for several years while his son Belshazzar remained in Babylon. Since then many more texts have come to light to confirm that Belshazzar ruled in Babylon during his father's absence. A Persian verse account of Nabonidus states:

> One camp he put into the charge of his eldest child,
> The troops he sent through the lands with himself.
> He struck his hands, he entrusted the kingship to him,

> While he himself set out on a far journey. . . .
> Towards Tema' in Amurru he set his face.
> He set out on a far journey, a road not within reach of old.
> They slew the king of Tema' with the sword. . . .
> That city he adorned, he made it . . .
> They made it like the palace of Babylon.[2]

When in 539 B.C. Cyrus was ready to march against Babylon, Nabonidus met him with his forces at Opis on the Tigris to prevent Cyrus from crossing the river. The Babylonians, however, suffered a disastrous defeat, and the Persians were able to push through to Sippar on the Euphrates. Cyrus captured this city without a fight on October 10, 539 B.C. According to the Babylonian Chronicle, Nabonidus fled south, while Belshazzar, who had stayed in Babylon, about 35 miles south of Sippar, remained in the capital, trusting in its strong fortifications. "It was here that, in a spirit of pride and arrogance and with a reckless feeling of security (*Prophets and Kings*, p. 523), he spent his last evening with his concubines and friends in frivolous drinking, using the sacred vessels of Solomon's Temple."[3] Daniel must have known Nabonidus, but he does not mention him by name because he played no part in the events recorded in chapter 5.

His Father Nebuchadnezzar—Six times the chapter calls Nebuchadnezzar Belshazzar's father (verses 2, 11 [three times], 13, 18), and one time it refers to Belshazzar as the son of Nebuchdnezzar (verse 22). But according to the ancient sources, Nabonidus was the father of Belshazzar. The problem is easily solved when we remember that the word "father" in Semitic languages, to which Hebrew and Aramaic belonged, can also mean grandfather, ancestor, or even predecessor. Neither language has specific terms for "grandfather" or "ancestor." The Black Obelisk of the Assyrian king Shalmaneser III refers to Jehu as the "son of Omri,"[4] although Jehu was not related to Omri. Rather he was one of his successors on the throne of Israel. Similarly Scripture describes Jesus as the "Son of David" (Matt. 1:1), even though David lived 1,000 years earlier than Christ. In the case of Belshazzar, some scholars assume that Nabonidus married one of the daughters of Nebuchadnezzar, which would have made the latter the grandfather of Belshazzar.[5]

Explanation

At the end of chapter 4 Nebuchadnezzar experienced a true conversion. Scripture gives no date for this event, but from historical records we know that Nebuchadnezzar died in 562 B.C. Following his death the Babylonians watched a series of weak kings come and go. Twenty-three years later, in 539 B.C., when Nabonidus, the last king of Babylon, sat on the throne, the events narrated in Daniel 5 took place. By then Daniel had been in Babylon for more than 60 years—he was now an old man.

The Handwriting on the Wall (Dan. 5:1-9)—As the chapter opens, we see a great banquet hall with 1,000 guests. In 1899, in one of the palaces of ancient Babylon, Robert Koldewey, who excavated the city, discovered a large hall (170 feet by 56 feet) that he identified as the throne room. "It is so clearly marked out for this purpose that no reasonable doubt can be felt as to its having been used as their principal audience chamber. If anyone should desire to localize the scene of Belshazzar's eventful banquet, he can surely place it with complete accuracy in this immense room."[6] Such feasts with thousands of guests were not unheard-of in ancient times. A stele discovered at Nimrud refers to a festival where King Ashurnasirpal II feasted 69,574 people during a 10-day period.[7] According to Esther 1:1-4 Xerxes I held a great feast for his officials that lasted 180 days. Such feasts involved much drinking, lewd singing, and unrestrained behavior. At the end of the evening (or early morning) guests would be helped home, to boast the next day that they had had a "good time."

Belshazzar's feast, however, never reached that point. We do not know what possessed him to request the sacred vessels that Nebuchadnezzar had brought from the Temple of Jerusalem (Dan. 1:2). Probably filled with wine, and no longer able to think clearly, he decided to do something unheard-of. He put the golden vessels from Jerusalem in the hands of his guests and led them in the revelry, singing praises to the gods of Babylon. As they boozed themselves, suddenly on the white plaster of the Great Hall the fingers of a man's hand appeared and began writing a message.

Instantly the laughter and singing stopped, and a stunned and petrified silence filled the room. The night of revelry became a night of revelation. Daniel notes that four things happened to Belshazzar: (1) his countenance changed, (2) his thoughts troubled him, (3) the joints of his hips loosened, and (4) his knees knocked against each other. In one brief moment the boastful king became a shivering, shaking, and hopeless mortal. He called for the astrologers, Chaldeans, and soothsayers, but instead of threatening them with death, as Nebuchadnezzar had done, he promised them great riches and honor. Yet in spite of the offers his advisers were baffled and unable to decipher the handwriting on the wall. This only increased the terror Belshazzar felt. It was now the third time that the wise men of Babylon had failed, and once more the stage had been set for Daniel to demonstrate the superiority of the followers of God.

Daniel to the Rescue (Dan. 5:10-24)—At that moment a queen entered the banquet hall. Scripture does not identify her, but she was not Belshazzar's wife, since his wives and concubines were already at the feast (verse 2). She must have been the queen mother. Many scholars believe "that she was Nitocris, daughter of Nebuchadnezzar, wife of Nabonidus and mother of Belshazzar."[8] In contrast to Belshazzar, who was beside himself with fright, the queen mother remained calm. She advised her son to pull himself together and reminded him that Daniel, who possessed "the Spirit of the Holy God," was still alive. "Let Daniel be called," she counseled (verses 11, 12). In describing Daniel's exceptional abilities she used the same words that her father, Nebuchadnezzar, had employed (cf. Dan. 5:11, 12 and 4:8, 9, 18).

When Daniel appeared, the king did not seem to recognize the former prime minister. "Are you that Daniel . . . ?" he asked. More than 20 years had elapsed since Nebuchadnezzar's death, at which time Daniel had probably retired from public service. Belshazzar now offers Daniel the third position of rulership in the kingdom, the first and second positions being occupied by his father and himself.

In his response Daniel first declines the king's gifts, then recounts the events of chapter 4 and explains to Belshazzar that Nebuchadnezzar's mental illness came as punishment for his pride, that Nebuchadnezzar had been a great king, but that in the end he had humbled himself before God. Then, having recounted the past, Daniel focuses on Belshazzar and delivers a stinging rebuke to the ruler. "You knew all this," he says to Belshazzar, "yet you refused to humble yourself" (see Dan. 5:22). Instead of learning from Nebuchadnezzar's experience, he had gone beyond what his grandfather had done, who took the holy vessels from the Temple in Jerusalem. Belshazzar had deliberately insulted and defied the living God by using the sacred vessels in praise of the pagan deities.

A Message From God (Dan. 5:25-29)—Now we learn for the first time what the writing on the wall actually said. In Aramaic the inscription, written without vowels, consisted of four words. How one read them depended on what vowels a person supplied. Without vowels they would have looked something like this: MN' MN' TQL WPRSN, the first word being written twice for emphasis. Daniel interpreted them as "mene, mene, teqel, upharsin" (the "w" represents the vowel "u," meaning "and"). To the king's advisers the words had not made sense. Some of them may have seen the names of three common weights on the wall—"a Mina, a Mina, a Shekel,[9] and a Half-shekel"—but what did (in more modern terms) "a stone, a stone, a pound, and half a pound" stand for?

"The three nouns listed in verse 25," observes Towner, "are treated as three passive verbs by Daniel in verses 26-28: MENE is related to the verb m-n-h, 'numbered'; TEKEL is related to the verb t-q-l-, 'weighed'; and PERES [the singular of pharsin] is constructed as the verb p-r-s, 'divided.'"[10] What the cryptic phrase said was "Numbered, numbered, weighed and divided." The last word, "peres," had a double connotation because the word for Persian *(paras)* has the same consonants as "peres." In his interpretation, therefore, Daniel said, "Your kingdom has been divided, and given to the Medes and Persians" (verse 28). As he said it, the Persians had already surrounded the city.

Despite Daniel's catastrophic explanation, Belshazzar kept his promise and bestowed great honor on Daniel. Perhaps he did not want to lose face in front of his courtiers by going back on his word. In any case, the honor lasted only a few hours. Babylon fell to the Persians that very night.

Historical Postscript (Dan. 5:30, 31)—Judgment came swiftly. Several ancient sources report that the Persians seized the city without a major battle.[11] Herodotus, who wrote some 80 years after the event, explained how the Persians penetrated the city's seemingly impregnable defenses: "Drawing off the river by a canal into the lake, which was till now a marsh, he [Cyrus] made the stream to sink till its former channel could be forded. When this happened, the Persians who were posted with this intent made their way into Babylon by the channel of the Euphrates, which had now sunk about to the height of the middle of a man's thigh. Now if the Babylonians had known beforehand or learnt what Cyrus was planning, they would have suffered the Persians to enter the city and brought them to a miserable end; for then they would have shut all the gates that opened on the river and themselves mounted up on to the walls that ran along the river banks, and so caught their enemies as in a trap. But as it was, the Persians were upon them unawares"[12] and so took the city. Xenophon adds that it was night when the Persians captured Babylon.[13]

That night the invading forces slew Belshazzar. Nabonidus, who had fled south, surrendered and committed himself to the mercy of Cyrus. "According to a Greek report, his life was spared by the generous Cyrus, and he was placed as vassal ruler over the distant land of Carmania."[14]

Application

What can Daniel 5 teach the modern reader? First, we can learn that no sin goes unpunished, and when sinners know that they shouldn't be doing something, the punishment will be even greater. In verses 22 and 23 Daniel presents Belshazzar with the divine accusation "You . . . have not humbled your heart. . . . You have lifted yourself up. . . . You have praised the gods of silver and gold." Machine-gun-like, Daniel uses the words "you" and "your" 14 times in the two verses. Belshazzar refused to learn from the experience of Nebuchadnezzar, and the result was a highly public judgment in the presence of his friends and family.

Second, we notice that God is deadly serious when it comes to holy things. Belshazzar wantonly profaned the sacred vessels from the Temple of Jerusalem, and by the end of the day he was dead. It reminds us of the immediate disastrous results of improper contact with holy things on other occasions. Uzzah put his hand out to steady the ark and fell dead (2 Sam. 6:6-9). Nadab and Abihu used unsanctified fire to burn incense, and the Lord struck them down (Lev. 10:1-3). King Uzziah usurped the place of the anointed priests and instantly became a leper (2 Chron. 26:16-21). We must not trifle with God. What He has declared holy, e.g., the Sabbath or the tithe, we should treat with reverence and care. God's Word is holy; therefore, "we should reverence God's Word. For the printed volume we should show respect, never putting it to common uses or handling it carelessly. And never should Scripture be quoted in a jest or paraphrased to point a witty saying."[15]

The common English expressions "Your days are numbered!" and "The handwriting is on the wall" are a modern legacy of Daniel 5, reminding people that judgment follows sin as night follows day.

---

[1] "According to P. A. Beaulieu, 37 archival texts dated from the first to the fourteenth year of Nabonidus now attest to Belshazzar's historicity" (Stephen R. Miller, *Daniel,* The New American Commentary [Broadman and Holman, 1994], vol. 18, p. 147).

[2] Sidney Smith, *Babylonian Historical Texts Relating to the Capture and Downfall of Babylon* (London: Menthuen, 1924), pp. 88, 89.

[3] *The Seventh-day Adventist Bible Commentary,* vol. 3, p. 49.

[4] I. M. Price, O. R. Sellers, and E. L. Carlson, *The Monuments and the Old Testament,* p. 240.

[5] G. L. Archer, "Daniel," p. 69. So also L. Wood, *A Commentary on Daniel* (Grand Rapids: Zondervan, 1973), p. 133.

[6] R. Koldewey, *The Excavations at Babylon* (London: Macmillan, 1914), p. 103.

[7] *The Seventh-day Adventist Bible Commentary,* vol. 4, p. 801.

[8] D. K. Campbell, *Daniel: Decoder of Dreams,* p. 60; cf. Archer, p. 72; Miller, p. 160.

[9] *Teqel* is the Aramaic form of *shekel.*

[10] W. Sibley Towner, *Daniel,* Interpretation (Atlanta: John Knox Press, 1984), p. 76.

[11] The Cyrus Cylinder says that Cyrus entered Babylon unopposed (*Ancient Near Eastern Texts,* ed. James B. Pritchard [Princeton, N.J.: Princeton University Press, 1969], pp. 315, 316). The Babylonian Chronicle also states that Cyrus entered Babylon on Tishri 16 (October 12, 539 B.C.) without a battle (*ibid.,* p. 306).

[12] Herodotus 1. 190, 191, in *Loeb Classical Library,* vol. 1, pp. 239-241. Xenophon confirms that Cyrus had the water of the Euphrates lowered and that his men entered the city in this way (*Cyropaedia* 7. 5. 9-24, in *Loeb Classical Library,* vol. 2, pp. 265-271).

[13] Xenophon *Cyropaedia,* 7. 5. 15, 16, in *Loeb Classical Library,* vol. 2, pp. 267-269.

[14] *The Seventh-day Adventist Bible Commentary,* vol. 3, p. 49.

[15] Ellen G. White, *Child Guidance* (Nashville: Southern Pub. Assn., 1954), pp. 538, 539.

CHAPTER 6

An Ancient Death Decree

Phodidas Ndamyumugabe, a Tutsi, was 24 years old when the Rwandan genocide of his people began in 1994. Like thousands of others, he had been hiding in the bushes when Hutu militia found him. After a short interrogation they decided to kill him, but first they ordered him to dig his own grave. As he dug Phodidas prayed, and God heard his prayer. When he had finished the grave the militia decided to use it for someone else they had just shot, and ordered him to excavate another one. Before starting the second grave, Phodidas asked, "Would you please give me my Bible so I may say something before digging my grave?" When the militia leader gave him permission, Phodidas began preaching to them about the great controversy. "This war is not about Hutus against Tutsis or Tutsis against Hutus," he explained, "because there are many Tutsis and Hutus who are not part of this. This war is between Jesus Christ and Satan." His 20-minute sermon left his listeners weeping. In the end they asked him to pray for them, then let him go. As a result, Phodidas was able to record his 36-day saga of miracle upon miracle in the book *Rwanda: Beyond Wildest Imagination*.[1] Like Daniel, Phodidas faced a death decree, and like Daniel, God delivered him from the killers' hands.

Information

Darius the Mede—At the end of Daniel 5 we encountered Darius the Mede as king of Babylon. Thus far, we have found no mention of any historical figure by that name in ancient documents. Liberal scholarship has concluded that Darius was an invention of the author, who, writing in the second century B.C., was not very familiar with sixth-century Babylonian history. Conservative scholars have proposed a number of identifications, but thus far have not reached any consensus. The prime contenders are: (1) Gubaru/Gobryas, the first governor of Babylon, and

53

(2) Cyrus the Great. Darius, some claim, was his throne name.

In favor of Gubaru is the fact that according to the Nabonidus Chronicle Cyrus appointed Gubaru as governor of Babylon. The Nabonidus Chronicle also reports that Gubaru installed subgovernors in Babylon (Dan. 6:2). Daniel 5:31 literally reads: "Darius the Mede received the kingdom." The passage can be interpreted to mean that Darius acquired the kingdom from a superior person, i.e., from Cyrus, as did Gubaru, governor of Babylon. Finally, Darius was 62 years old (verse 31), and from Xenophon we know that Gubaru was "well advanced in years."[2]

In favor of Cyrus is the fact that dual titles were not uncommon in ancient times.[3] Darius could have been Cyrus's Median throne name. The ancient Jewish translations (LXX and Theodotion) endorse this identification by using the name Cyrus rather than Darius in Daniel 11:1. Thus D. J. Wiseman translates Daniel 6:28 as "Daniel prospered in the reign of Darius, even (namely, or i.e.) the reign of Cyrus the Persian."[4] In 539 B.C. Cyrus would have been about 62 years of age. His father's name was Cambyses. The name Ahasuerus in "Darius the son of Ahasuerus" (Dan. 9:1), therefore, is understood to be an ancient royal title rather than the actual name of Cyrus's father. Since the evidence in both cases is not decisive, hopefully we will discover further historical data that will clarify the matter.

Satraps—The Persian term *satrap,* meaning "protector of the kingdom," could refer to provincial rulers or kings, as well as to lower royal officials. According to the Behistun inscription from the time of Darius I (521-486), the empire was divided into 23 satrapies.[5] The fifth satrapy included Phoenicia, Palestine, and Cyprus.[6] Since Darius the Mede in Daniel 6 ruled only over the kingdom of Babylon, the 120 satraps most likely were royal officials who had charge of smaller divisions within his realm.

The Laws of the Medes and Persians—Esther 1:19; 8:8 also mentions the immutability of "the laws of the Persians and the Medes," and Diodorus Siculus (17. 30) seems to refer to it when he comments that "Darius III could not repeal a death sentence passed on an innocent man."[7]

Explanation
The Plot Against Daniel (Dan. 6:1-9)—Daniel not only survived the downfall of Babylon, but Darius elevated him to a high position in his new government. Scripture does not tell us how Darius heard of Daniel, but his service under Nebuchadnezzar and the handwriting-on-the-wall episode must have come to the Mede's attention. Recognizing Daniel's extraordinary administrative skills, Darius determined to make him his prime minister.

The king doubtless acted in the best interests of the state, but he failed to take into account the feelings of jealousy among his top officials. To place a former prime minister of the defeated Babylonians in a position that according to their expectations should be theirs was too much for them. The politicians, therefore, ordered their legal sleuths to "dig for dirt" in Daniel's character, but they couldn't find any skeletons in his closet, because he was faithful "concerning the kingdom" (verse 4). Exposing and slandering others has obviously been a favored method since ancient times to bring down the opposition.

Having failed to discover anything in Daniel's character or professional activities that they could use to discredit him with Darius, the governors and satraps turned to his religion. Since his religious life and the performance of his duties did not conflict with each other, they had to invent something. Knowing that Daniel was a strict monotheist who prayed to his God three times a day, they used the knowledge to set their trap.

Their claim before Darius that all the governors, administrators, satraps, counselors, and advisers had consulted together was greatly exaggerated. The majority were probably scattered across the kingdom and did not even know what was going on. But their flattery achieved its purpose. The king took their bait.

The decree forbade people to petition "any god or man for thirty days." Daniel's enemies were confident that 30 days was long enough to trap him, and he did not disappoint them.

Daniel's Faithfulness (Dan. 6:10-18)—His enemies made sure that Daniel soon learned of the new law, but he firmly decided to continue his habit of praying three times daily, "as was his custom." Did Daniel consider the alternatives? Close the shutters and pray in secret, or cease praying for 30 days and outwit the plotters. After all, couldn't he serve his people better if he stayed alive? Why make an issue of being seen in prayer? We don't know if he spent any time at all considering the alternatives. What we do know is that anything else but following his usual practice was unacceptable to him. It would have involved the loss of his public testimony of his faith in the God of Israel.

Solomon's prayer at the dedication of the Temple (1 Kings 8:35, 38, 44, 48) repeatedly mentions prayer facing Jerusalem and the Temple. Scripture has no command to pray three times a day, but we know from Psalm 55:17 that David prayed "evening and morning and at noon." We do not know how widespread a custom it was in Old Testament times, but according to the Didache the early church practiced it.[8]

When it became clear that Daniel was not obeying the king's decree, the plotters hurried to report him to the king. Knowing the king's sympathy for Daniel, they first made sure that the monarch clearly understood the law he had signed before they told him the news. Immediately realizing that he had been duped, Darius was extremely upset. Since the law could not be changed, he had to condemn Daniel to the lions' den, yet he did everything he could think of to save his aged counselor.

When the time came, the king personally accompanied Daniel to the lions' den while bemoaning his own stupidity. His only hope now was that the prisoner's God would step in and deliver His servant, as he had delivered Daniel's three friends from the fiery furnace. The soldiers secured the stone over the opening of the den, and the king and his nobles sealed it with their signet rings so that no one should tamper with it, either to rescue Daniel or to harm him should the lions decide to fast.

Daniel's Rescue (Dan. 6:19-24)—At dawn, as early as possible, the king hastened to the den. Lacocque suggests that "perhaps we should see the king's hasty return early the next morning (verse 20) in the perspective of the ancient Babylonian custom that the victim would be pardoned if he were tortured and had not died by the following day."[9] In any case, Darius must have had some glimmer of hope that Daniel had survived the night. Arriving at the mouth of the den, he called out to Daniel in anguish and hope, and, we can be sure, was overjoyed when he heard the voice of his trusted servant announce, "My God sent His angel and stopped the lions' mouths." The angel here plays the same role as the fourth man in the blazing furnace in chapter 3.

If anyone wondered whether the lions were actually hungry and ready to kill, Daniel 6:24 dispels any doubt. When the guards threw Daniel's accusers and their families into the den, the lions pounced on them and crushed their bones before they even reached the bottom of the pit, thereby providing evidence that the deliverance of Daniel was a miraculous event.

We recoil with horror when we read of women and children being fed to the lions, but the king acted in a fashion typical of despots of his day. Herodotus testifies that consigning to death whole families along with condemned men was in accordance with Persian custom. "[Darius] seized Intaphrenes with his sons and all his household—for he much suspected that the man was plotting a rebellion with his kinsfolk. . . . [Except for the wife, her oldest son, and her brother] all the rest he put to death."[10]

Application

What captures our attention in this chapter is Daniel's steadfastness and loyalty to God in the face of death. He had stood for principles as a teenager (Dan. 1), and he refused to give in to threats when he was an old man. Some of the qualities that distinguished Daniel were:

1. *Wisdom:* Daniel and his three friends, in their youth, received divine wisdom (Dan. 1:17). Daniel used his gift well. The queen in chapter 5, therefore, described him as one possessing insight "like the wisdom of the gods."

2. *Altruism:* Repeatedly in the first six chapters we find Daniel displaying consideration for others. To protect the chief steward, he asked for a test of only 10 days (Dan. 1:10-13). He was concerned for the wise men of Babylon (Dan. 2:24) and for King Nebuchadnezzar (Dan. 4:19).

3. *Integrity:* Both Nebuchadnezzar and Darius recognized that they could trust Daniel, that neither race, rank, nor wealth could sway him from his faithfulness to God (Dan. 2:48; 5:29; 6:3). In every situation he sought to be just, fair, and merciful.

4. *Education:* Daniel was not only instructed in the affairs of his own people but had received a thorough training in the university of Babylon. He spoke their language, and those with whom he came in contact could have confidence that he knew his business.

5. *Experience:* At the time of the events in chapter 6 Daniel was more than 80 years old. His life of faithful service at a pagan court had demonstrated that his experience as a statesman, who walked closely with his God, was invaluable.

Daniel's experience in chapter 6 reminds us that a governmental decree in the future will require all humanity to worship the beast and his image (Rev. 13:11-15). Governmental pressure to conform to human laws contrary to those of God's laws will reveal the strength of character of professed Christians in the final days of earth's history. Many will cave in and join those on the highway to eternal destruction, while others will stand firm as did Daniel, and shine like the stars in heaven's firmament.

"From the story of Daniel's deliverance we may learn that in seasons of trial and gloom God's children should be just what they were when their prospects were bright with hope and their surroundings all that they could desire. Daniel in the lions' den was the same Daniel who stood before the king as chief among the ministers of state and as a prophet of the Most High. A man whose heart is stayed upon God will be the same in the hour of his greatest trial as he is in prosperity, when the light and favor of God and of man beam upon him."[11]

---

[1] Phodidas Ndamyumugabe, *Rwanda: Beyond Wildest Imagination* (Berrien Springs,

Mich.: Lesley Books, 2000), pp. 101-118.

[2] Xenophon *Cryopaedia* 4. 6. 1, in *Loeb Classical Library,* vol. 2, p. 391.

[3] For example, in 2 Kings 15:19 Pul is the Babylonian throne name for the Assyrian king Tiglath-pileser III (745-727 B.C.). Cf. 1 Chron. 5:26.

[4] D. J. Wiseman, *Notes on Some Problems in the Book of Daniel* (London: Tyndale, 1970), p. 12. He considers the *waw* to be a *waw* explicative ("that is"), as it clearly is in 1 Chronicles 5:26.

[5] André Lacocque, *The Book of Daniel* (Atlanta: John Knox Press, 1979), p. 109. According to Esther 1:1, Xerxes (485-465 B.C.) organized his empire into 127 provinces.

[6] Herodotus 3. 91, in *Loeb Classical Library,* vol. 2, p. 119.

[7] Ernest Lucas, *Daniel,* Apollos Old Testament Commentary (Downers Grove, Ill.: InterVarsity Press, 2002), p. 150.

[8] Didache 8. 3, in Edgar J. Goodspeed, *The Apostolic Fathers* (London: Independent Press, Ltd., 1950), p. 15. The Church Fathers greatly valued the book *The Teaching (Gr. didache) of the Twelve Apostles,* written most likely in the second century A.D.

[9] Lacocque, p. 118.

[10] Herodotus 3. 119, 121, in *Loeb Classical Library,* vol. 2, pp. 147-149.

[11] E. G. White, *Prophets and Kings,* p. 545.

CHAPTER 7

Daniel's History Lesson

In Daniel 7, which is a transitional chapter, we turn from the historical accounts of the prophet's life to his visions. Its use of the Aramaic language and its parallelism with chapter 2 connect it with the preceding chapters while its subject matter binds it to what follows. The great prophetic panorama it describes came to Daniel about 553 B.C., the first year of Belshazzar's coregency with his father, Nabonidus (Dan. 7:1).

The chapter focuses on the power represented by the symbol of the little horn. Seven out of 28 verses deal with its activities. Four wild beast symbols that parallel the four metal empires of the image that Nebuchadnezzar saw in a dream in Daniel 2 precede its appearance. Both chapters conclude with the appearance of God's kingdom.

Information

Animal Symbolism—Scripture employs animal symbols to represent various powers in history. Jeremiah uses both the lion and the eagle to represent Nebuchadnezzar (Jer. 49:19-22). Elsewhere, Scripture compares Egypt to a heifer (Jer. 46:20), a lion (Eze. 32:2), and a crocodile or dragon (Eze. 29:3). Egyptian iconography symbolizes the king as a lion on a number of stamp seals and scarabs. And numerous Persian coins from the fourth century B.C. depict the Persian king as victor over a rampant lion. "One cannot escape the temptation to consider this particular imagery as a forceful hint at the defeat of the Babylonians by the succeeding Persian empire."[1]

The Rise of the Papacy—The early Christian emperors considered themselves rather than the bishop of Rome to be the true rulers of the church. The emperors Constantine the Great and Theodosius called the First and Second Ecumenical Councils of Christian bishops in Nicea (A.D. 325) and Constantinople (A.D. 381) without reference to the bishop of Rome. To counteract the influence of the emperors, Pope Siricius (384-

399) formulated the first proclamation of the right and duty of the bishop of Rome to rule over the whole of Christendom: "We (the Successors of Peter) carry on our shoulders the burdens of all who are weighed down," he wrote. "Indeed, in our person the blessed Apostle Peter himself carries these burdens—he who regards us as the *heir to his administration*. . . . No priest of the Lord is free to ignore the decision of the Apostolic See."[2]

Over the next two centuries the popes in Rome became more and more adamant in their insistence that they rather than the emperors should be the final arbiters in church affairs. When Attila the Hun threatened Rome, Leo I (440-461) confronted the "Scourge of God" and won. He somehow persuaded Attila to abandon his quest for the Eternal City, a fact that greatly enhanced the prestige of the bishop of Rome. History will record that it was Leo the Great who laid the foundations of the political power of the popes. Earlier in the century the illustrious Augustine, bishop of Hippo in North Africa, had uttered the now-famous words *"Roma locuta, causa finita"* (Rome has spoken; the case is closed). The doctrine that Christ had granted papal power to Peter and that he passed it on to his successors in Rome began to take firm root. The creation of the Papal States in the eighth century and the fact that the Muslims conquered the Christian centers of Alexandria, Jerusalem, and Antioch, reducing their influence, further enhanced the stature and importance of the bishop of Rome.

The power of the Papacy reached its zenith under Gregory VII (1073-1085), who first enforced the theory that the pope could depose kings, and under Innocent III (1198-1216), who made himself absolute sovereign of Italy, requiring all officials in Rome to take an oath to him.

The Year-Day Principle

Throughout most of church history people have interpreted apocalyptic time prophecies according to the historicist method of interpretation. Only in the past 200 years have other systems, such as preterism and futurism, replaced historicism as the dominant method of interpreting the books of Daniel and Revelation. Seventh-day Adventists, however, have remained historicists, and they continue to use the year-day principle that forms the backbone of historicism. We can summarize the main points in support of it as follows:

1. Since the visions in Daniel 7 and 8 are largely symbolic, with a number of different beasts representing important historical empires (7:3-7; 8:3-5, 20, 21), the time periods (7:25; 8:14) should also be seen as symbolic.

2. The fact that the visions deal with the rise and fall of known em-

pires in history that existed for hundreds of years indicates that the prophetic time periods must also cover long time periods.

3. The peculiar way in which Daniel expresses the time periods—"time, times, and half a time" (Dan. 7:25; 12:7)—indicates that we should not take them literally.

4. In Daniel 7 the little-horn power follows the four beasts, which together account for a reign of at least 1,000 years. The horn is the focus of the vision, since it is most directly in opposition to God. Three and a half literal years for the struggle between the little horn and the Most High are out of proportion to the comprehensive scope of salvation history portrayed in the entire vision.

5. According to the context, the expressions "time, times, and half a time" (Dan. 7:25; 12:7; Rev. 12:14), "forty-two months" (Rev. 11:2; 13:5), and "one thousand two hundred and sixty days" (Rev. 11:3; 12:6) all apply to the same time period, but the natural expression "three years and six months" does not appear even once. "The Holy Spirit seems, in a manner, to exhaust all the phrases by which the interval could be expressed, excluding always that one form, which would be used of course in ordinary writing, and is used invariably in Scripture on other occasions, to denote the literal period. This variation is most significant, if we accept the year-day system, but quite inexplicable on the other view."[4]

6. The prophecies in Daniel 7 and 8, and 10-12 lead up to the "time of the end" (Dan. 8:17; 11:35, 40; 12:4, 9), which is followed by the resurrection (Dan. 12:2) and the setting up of God's everlasting kingdom (Dan. 7:27). "In the sweep of history described in these prophecies that extends from the prophet in the sixth century B.C. to our time and beyond, literal time periods of only 3 to 6 years are not capable of reaching anywhere near this final end time. Therefore, these prophetic time periods should be seen as symbolic and standing for considerable longer periods of actual historical time extending to the end of time."[5]

7. The only commonly used measure of time not employed in the prophecies of Daniel and Revelation is the year. The prophetic passages refer to days, weeks, and months, but not the time unit "year." The most obvious explanation is that the "year" is the unit symbolized by everything else throughout the prophecies.

8. In Numbers 14:34 and Ezekiel 4:6 God deliberately employed the day-for-a-year principle as a teaching device.

9. In Daniel 9:24-27 the 70-weeks time prophecy met its fulfillment at the exact time if we use the year-day principle to interpret it. Many in-

terpreters, who in other apocalyptic texts do not employ the year-day principle, recognize that the 70 weeks are in fact "weeks of years" reaching from the Persian period to the time of Christ. Thus the pragmatic test in Daniel 9 confirms the validity of the year-day principle.

Explanation

The Vision of the Four Beasts (Dan. 7:1-7)—The symbols in this vision are familiar to all Bible students. Winds represent storms of war and conquest (Jer. 25:31-33; 49:36, 37; Zech. 7:14; Rev. 7:1), and the sea or water stands regularly for people and nations (Isa. 17:12, 13; 57:20; Jer. 46:6-8; Rev. 17:15). The picture suggests that the rise and fall of empires results from revolutions and wars.

According to Daniel 7:17, the four beasts represent four kings, or kingdoms, "which arise out of the earth." Except for the added detail of the little horn in Daniel 7, the visions in Daniel 2 and 7 portray the same sequence of kingdoms and historical events.[6]

	Daniel 2	Daniel 7
Babylon	Head of gold	Winged lion
Medo-Persia	Chest and arms of silver	Bear
Greece	Belly and thighs of bronze	Leopard with four heads
Rome	Legs of iron	Dreadful beast
Divided Europe	Feet of iron and clay	10 horns
Papacy	—	Little horn
Second Advent	Stone cut without hands	Saints receive the kingdom

Babylon: The winged lion was a particularly appropriate symbol of Babylon. Representations of lions appear on the walls of the great processional way to the Ishtar Gate as well as the gate itself. They occur also on the outer wall of the throne room in Babylon. In the vision Daniel saw that the lion's "wings were plucked off" (Dan. 7:4), indicating the fact that after Nebuchadnezzar had completed his immense program of conquest and reconstruction his successors settled down in the way so typical of "a man's heart" to enjoy the wealth and luxury they had inherited.

Medo-Persia: The lopsided bear crunching three ribs represents the empire of Medo-Persia and its conquest of Lydia (547 B.C.), Babylon (539 B.C.), and Egypt (525 B.C.) under the leadership of Cyrus and Cambyses. Under Darius Hystaspes and Xerxes the Persian Empire attempted to conquer Greece, but the Greeks defeated them at Marathon (490 B.C.) and again at Salamis (480 B.C.) and Platea (479 B.C.).

Greece: The leopard has a reputation for its swiftness and agility. The four wings are a fitting symbol for the speed of movement characteristic of the young Alexander, who set out in 334 B.C. with 35,000 men and who in 10 years established the greatest empire the Near East had known up to that time. The leopard, Daniel reported, had four heads, which in Scripture sometimes represent rulers or governments (Dan. 2:38; Isa. 7:8, 9). Daniel here predicted that the empire of Greece would fragment into four kingdoms. From history we know that when Alexander died, his generals began to fight among themselves. Out of their struggle emerged in 301 B.C. four separate kingdoms: Seleucus took Asia from Phrygia to India; western Asia Minor and Thrace fell to Lysimachus; Ptolemy became king of Egypt; and Cassander established himself on the throne of Greece and Macedonia.

Rome: The fourth kingdom, Rome, was different from all the others before it in that they had been monarchies, whereas Rome began with a nonmonarchial form of government. Founded in the year 753 B.C., the city of Rome early became a republic, and during the Hellenistic age it first conquered all of Italy and then began to reach out and participate in Hellenistic affairs. It became the ruling world power when in 168 B.C., at the Battle of Pydna, the Roman general Aemilius Paulus won a complete victory over Perseus of Macedonia.

The fourth beast had 10 horns (Dan. 7:7). Corresponding to the mingling of the iron with the clay in the feet and toes of the image, they represent the nations that emerged from the Roman Empire and to a large extent maintained its civilization. Though many interpreters have tried to identify exactly 10 peoples and 10 kingdoms descending from them, it is best to take the number 10 as a round figure (e.g., Gen. 31:7; Num. 14:22; 1 Sam. 1:8; etc.), indicating a multiplicity of states in contrast to the one empire of Rome.

The Little Horn (Dan. 7:8)—From our study thus far, we have seen that the fourth beast is Rome and that the 10 horns symbolize the division of the one Roman Empire into many different nations. But which power does the little horn represent? Church history indicates that only one power in history fits the description of the little horn—the Roman Catholic Church. "Out of the ruins of political Rome arose the great moral Empire in the 'giant form' of the Roman Church."[7]

The great German church historian Adolf von Harnack explains that

63

the Roman Church "pushed itself into the place of the Roman World-Empire, of which it is the actual continuation; the empire has not perished, but has only undergone a transformation. . . . The Roman Church is the old Roman Empire consecrated by the Gospel."[8]

The three horns that were "plucked up" "before it" were the Arian powers of the Heruli, the Vandals, and the Ostrogoths. Arius, a priest in Alexandria, taught that Christ was a created being. Although the Council of Nicea (A.D. 325) condemned his teaching, nevertheless, it continued to grow, and when the Germanic invaders converted to Christianity it was mostly to the Arian form. The bishop of Rome, however, was a Trinitarian who accepted the divinity of Christ. Daniel 7:8 indicates that these powers were to be uprooted so that the Papacy could develop and assert itself. The Ostrogoths defeated the Heruli in Italy in A.D. 493, and they in turn succumbed to the armies of Justinian, the emperor in Constantinople, in A.D. 538 and were completely destroyed in A.D. 554. Justinian defeated the third power, the Vandals, in A.D. 534. "Thus the three Arian nations who refused to renounce their heretical faith were uprooted or subdued and the other Arian peoples turned orthodox, leaving the bishop of Rome the undisputed ruler of nations and the corrector of heretics."[9]

We can illustrate the "pompous words" of the little horn by some of the pronouncements and claims made by the popes and councils of the Roman Catholic Church. As late as 1894 Pope Leo XIII (1878-1903) claimed in his encyclical "The Reunion of Christendom" that "we hold upon this earth the place of God Almighty."[10]

The Vision Interpreted (Dan. 7:15-25)—When a heavenly figure interprets the vision, he tells Daniel that the saints will fall into the hands of the little horn for three and a half times, and that the little horn will intend to change times and laws (verse 25).

The persecution of faithful Christians by ecclesiastical authorities throughout the Middle Ages is well known in history. Tens of thousands of innocent Christians perished under the Inquisition. On Saint Bartholomew's Day in 1572 alone thousands of Huguenots perished in France, for which Pope Gregory XIII returned solemn thanks to heaven.

While no one can really change God's times and laws, a shift in the weekly day of worship did occur during the first four centuries of church history. To distance themselves from Judaism, Christians substituted characteristic Jewish religious observances such as Passover and the Sabbath with Easter Sunday and the weekly Sunday. The Council of Laodicea (between A.D. 343 and A.D. 381), the first church council to enjoin Sunday observance, said in canon 29 that "Christians shall not Judaize and be idle on Saturday, but shall work on that day; but the Lord's day [Sunday] they shall especially honour, and, as being Christians, shall, if possible, do no work on that day. If, however, they are found Judaizing, they shall be shut out [Greek *anathema*] from Christ."[11] Since then many other Sunday laws have appeared.

Daniel 12:7 again mentions the time period of three and one half times, or three and one half prophetic years, and the book of Revelation refers to it in various ways:

Dan. 7:25	A time, and times, and the dividing of time
Dan. 12:7	A time, times, and a half
Rev. 11:2	Forty and two months
Rev. 11:3	A thousand two hundred and threescore days
Rev. 12:6	A thousand two hundred and threescore days
Rev. 12:14	A time, and times, and half a time
Rev. 13:5	Forty and two months

A comparison of the preceding texts shows that a prophetic year has 360 days; thus three and one half years is the same as 1260 prophetic days or 42 prophetic months. According to the year-day principle of prophetic interpretation, the three and one half prophetic years or 1260 days refer to the time of papal dominion from the sixth to the end of the eighteenth century, specifically to the time period from A.D. 538 to 1798.

In A.D. 533 Emperor Justinian, who resided in Constantinople, recognized the bishop of Rome rather than the patriarch of Constantinople, who perhaps was too near to him for comfort, as head of all the churches both West and East. Five years later, in A.D. 538, Justinian's general Belisarius delivered Rome from the siege of the Ostrogoths. Thus the formal recognition of the bishop of Rome as "the head of all the Holy Churches"[12] in practical terms became effective in A.D. 538. Thereafter, beginning with the Franks, the other Germanic tribes became Catholic Christians, and replaced the emperor of the East as the political support of the Papacy.

On November 9, 1793, the French Revolution abolished Christianity and replaced it with the worship of reason. Nearly five years later, on February 10, 1798, Napoleon's general Berthier entered Rome and took Pope Pius VI prisoner. Though the Papacy continued, its power had lessened, and it has never since wielded the same kind or measure of authority that it did during the 1260 prophetic days. Although during the French Revolution the pope lost the Papal States, the Congress of Vienna (1815) restored his secular, or political, power. Then in 1860 the armies of Victor Emmanuel II seized the Papal States (except Rome itself) and annexed them to Italy. Ten years later, on September 20, 1870, the forces of Victor Emmanuel II entered Rome, and a year later Rome became the capital of the united kingdom of Italy. The secular political power the Papacy had formally exercised for more than 1,000 years came to an end, and the pope voluntarily became "the prisoner of the Vatican" until he regained his temporal power from Mussolini in 1929.

Application

While the vision of the four beasts and the little horn may have given some people nightmares, it contains some vital lessons for God's people living in the time of the end:

1. Prophecy Is the Foundation of Our Faith.—The apostle Peter wrote that "we have the prophetic word made more sure" (2 Peter 1:19, RSV). The fulfillment of the messianic prophecies in the life of Christ provided an unshakable foundation for Christian faith. Similarly, the completion of the prophecies of Daniel 7 in the history of the world since Nebuchadnezzar confirms for every believer the truthfulness of the Word of God. Hence, we dare not ignore it. Ellen White admonishes every minister to "present the sure word of prophecy as the foundation of the faith of Seventh-day Adventists."[13]

2. The Prophetic Word Is Important.—The fact that Daniel 7 repeats the prophecy of the four world empires and the kingdom of God in Daniel 2 under different symbols indicates that God saw its message as something highly important for His people to know. We are a prophetic movement, and "the people are to be educated," Ellen White says, "to read the sure word of prophecy in the light of the living oracles. They need to know that the signs of the times are fulfilling."[14]

3. God Is in Control.—Chapter 7 also teaches us that in spite of the apparent chaos in our world at times, God is still in control. Daniel predicted four world empires, the activities of the little horn, and the kingdom of the saints. The fulfillment of the first two elements of the prophecy indicates His foreknowledge. Thus we can have confidence that the predicted third event, the giving of the kingdom to the saints, will also take place. The sure word of prophecy provides us with the hope of good things to come—an everlasting kingdom in which Christ will reign supreme.

[1] Jürg Eggler, "Iconographic Motifs From Palestine/Israel and Daniel 7:2-14" (unpublished D.Litt. dissertation, University of Stellenbosch, June 1998), p. 292.

[2] Denzinger Schönmetzer, *Enchridion Symbolorum, Definitionum et Declarationum* (Rome: Herder, 1965), p. 72, in Ian Guthridge, *The Rise and Decline of the Christian Empire* (Middle Park, Victoria, Australia: Medici School/Publications), p. 78.

[3] For this summary the writer acknowledges his indebtedness to appendix F in Desmond Ford, *Daniel* (Nashville: Southern Pub. Assn., 1978), pp. 300-305.

[4] Thomas R. Birks, *First Elements of Sacred Prophecy* (London: William E. Painter, 1843), p. 352.

[5] William H. Shea, *Selected Studies on Prophetic Interpretation,* rev. ed., Daniel and Revelation Committee Series (Silver Spring, Md.: Biblical Research Institute, 1992), vol. 1, p. 73.

[6] The identification of the four beasts with Babylon, Medo-Persia, Greece, and Rome goes back to the early Church Fathers (see Hippolytus *Treatise on Christ and Anitchrist* 23-28, in *Ante-Nicene Fathers,* vol. 5, pp. 209, 210; *Jerome's Commentary on Daniel,* trans. G. L. Archer, Jr. [Grand Rapids: Baker Book House, 1958], pp. 72-75).

[7] Alexander C. Flick, *The Rise of the Mediaeval Church* (New York: Burt Franklin, 1959), p. 150.

[8] Adolf von Harnack, *What Is Christianity?* trans. Thomas B. Saunders (New York: Putnam, 1903), p. 270.

[9] Taylor G. Bunch, *The Book of Daniel* (Payson, Ariz.: Leaves-of-Autumn Books, 1991), p. 101.

[10] *The Great Encyclical Letters of Pope Leo XIII* (New York: Benziger, 1903), p. 304.

[11] Joseph Hefele, *A History of the Councils of the Church,* trans. and ed. H. N. Oxenham (Edinburgh: T. and T. Clark, 1896), vol. 2, p. 316.

[12] Code of Justinian, book 1, title 1, 8; titled 1, 4 in P. Scott, *The Civil Law* (Cincinnati: Central Trust Company, 1932), vol. 12, p. 12, in Don F. Neufeld, ed., *Seventh-day Adventist Bible Students' Handbook* (Washington, D.C.: Review and Herald Pub. Assn., 1962), no. 1134.

[13] Ellen G. White, *Evangelism* (Washington, D.C.: Review and Herald Pub. Assn., 1946), p. 196.

[14] White, *Testimonies for the Church,* vol. 7, p. 158.

CHAPTER 8

The Pre-Advent Judgment

Some see the Seventh-day Adventist understanding of the pre-Advent investigative judgment, described in Daniel 7:9-14, as the unique Adventist contribution to biblical theology.[1] One or more of the other churches or denominations, either past or present, share the other fundamental beliefs of the church. Some, therefore, have called the doctrine a face-saving device "to compensate for errors in prophetic interpretation."[2] A study of this topic, however, will show that Seventh-day Adventists do not alone teach the concept of a pre-Advent judgment, and that strong biblical support exists for it.

Information

The Ancient of Days (Dan. 7:9)—This is the only verse in the Bible that depicts God the Father in human form. It portrays Him as an old and therefore wise human judge sitting in His courtroom. The white garment, symbolizing the absolute moral purity of the divine judge (Isa. 1:18), reminds us of the white robes worn by the 24 elders around the throne of God (Rev. 4:4) and the white garments the saints shall wear one day (Rev. 3:5). The white hair symbolizes wisdom and old age which in the biblical world would best qualify Him as judge (Lev. 19:32; Job 32:7). The depiction of God's throne as a flame of fire with burning wheels represents divine judgment (Ps. 50:3, 4).

The Son of Man (Dan. 7:13)—In Ezekiel God uses the phrase "son of man" more than 70 times to address the prophet (Eze. 2:1, 3; 3:1, 3, 4, 10, etc.). It emphasizes the limitations of Ezekiel's humanity in contrast to the divine majesty.

Commentators have interpreted the Danielic "Son of man" as the archangel Michael,[3] the personification of the people of God, the Jewish nation,[4] and as the Messiah. The messianic view is the oldest and most prevailing interpretation among Jews and Christians.[5] In the book of Enoch, written late during the intertestamental period, the "Son of man" is a messianic figure "to whom belongs righteousness," who deposes "kings and the mighty ones from their comfortable seats,"[6] and who brings about the end of the present age. The Gospels present "Son of man" as Jesus' favorite title to refer to Himself. He used it more than 80 times to identify Himself (1) as the earthly Son of man who is presently at work (Mark 2:10, 28), (2) as the Son of man who will suffer, die, and rise again (Matt. 17:22, 23; 20:18, 19), and (3) as the Son of man who will come again in eschatological glory (Matt. 24:30; 26:64).[7] As used by Jesus, the title reminded His hearers of the Danielic "Son of man" who received dominion, glory, and an everlasting kingdom (Dan. 7:14).

Explanation

Daniel 7 consists essentially of a vision, its interpretation, and the prophet's reaction to the vision. A prologue (verses 1, 2) and an epilogue (verse 28) frame the chapter. The vision (verses 2-14) depicts four beasts, with the focus on the fourth beast, which has 10 horns, from which arises another little horn. The little horn becomes the main opposition to the "Most High" and the saints in the rest of the chapter. While the activities of the little horn continue here on earth, Daniel has his attention drawn to a heavenly judgment scene (verses 9-14) that condemns the little horn, vindicates the saints, and gives dominion, glory, and a kingdom to "one like the Son of Man" (verse 13).

The judgment passage in Daniel 7:9-14 contains three scenes: (a) a judgment in heaven in verses 9 and 10; (b) the end of the fourth beast, i.e., the outcome of the judgment in verses 11 and 12; and (c) the reception of the kingdom by Son of man (Christ) in verses 13 and 14.

The Court Was Seated, and the Books Were Opened (Dan. 7:9, 10)—Many people love courtroom scenes as long as they are not sitting in the seat of the accused. Generally, the picture of a judge in court conjures up the ideas of a crime committed and punishment meted out. Most people, therefore, feel apprehensive when called to jury duty or to stand in the witness box. Scripture, however, "sees judgment from the viewpoint of the oppressed, the suffering victim, and thus places it in the context of salvation and victory over the oppressor and evil."[8] As a result, the Bible sometimes describes judges as deliverers or saviors (Judges 3:9, 15; 18:28).

The concept of an investigate judgment, as taught by Seventh-day Adventists, is not foreign to the Bible. Repeatedly in the Old as well as in the New Testament we come across investigative judgments. Right from the beginning of God's dealing with sinners in Genesis 3 a pattern of judicial procedure emerges. First comes the investigation: "Where are you?" "Who told you?" "Have you eaten from the tree?" (Gen. 3:9-11). Following His investigation God announces the verdict in verses 14-19. We find a similar situation in God's dealing with Cain (Gen. 4:9, 10) and in His handling of Sodom and Gomorrah. Most of Genesis 18 and 19 describes God's investigations and deliberations prior to His punitive act. It is significant that the New Testament projects the judgment on Sodom and Gomorrah as an "example," or a "type," of God's judgment at the end (2 Peter 2:6; Jude 7). The writings of Israel's prophets depict God arraying Israel or the nations before His judgment seat, His making an investigation, the stating of facts, the summoning of witnesses, and finally the pronouncement of a verdict (e.g., Isa. 5:1-7; 43:8-13, 22-28). The sequence is always the same: sin, investigation, and judgment.[9]

The concept of a pre-Advent investigative judgment appears also in the New Testament. The parable of the wedding feast in Matthew 22 is a prime example. "When the king came in to see the guests, he saw a man there who did not have on a wedding garment" (verse 11). The king's inspection of the guests represents a process of investigation. It determined who of the guests could remain and who could not. In this sense it is a picture of the investigative pre-Advent judgment in heaven going on now.

Other New Testament texts that presuppose a pre-Advent judgment are John 5:28, 29, in which John mentions a resurrection for life and a resurrection for condemnation, and Revelation 20:4-6. Many biblical exegetes agree that Revelation 20 teaches two literal resurrections of the dead separated by 1,000 years. Inasmuch as only the "blessed and holy" rise in the first resurrection, a prior judgment must have taken place to determine who will take part. Non-Adventist theologians have also recognized this. Lutheran Joseph A. Seiss, for example, wrote: "The resurrection, and the changes which pass 'in the twinkling of an eye' upon the living, are themselves the fruits and embodiments of antecedent judgment. They are the consequences of adjudications then already made. Strictly speaking, men are neither raised nor translated, in order to come to judgment. Resurrections and translations are products of judgment previously passed, upon the dead as dead, and upon the quick as quick. 'The dead in Christ shall rise first,' because they are already adjudged to be in Christ, and the living saints are caught up together with them to the clouds, because they are already adjudged to be saints, and worthy to attain that world."[10]

In Revelation 14 the first angel's message, "Fear God and give glory to Him, for the hour of His judgment has come" (verse 7), precedes the harvest of the earth (verses 14-20). The sequence of events in this chapter clearly indicates that the judgment spoken of in verse 7 takes place before the execution of the judgment at Christ's second advent in verses 14-20.[11] Thus throughout Scripture we find the concept of an investigative judgment, as depicted in Daniel 7, prior to the Second Advent.

The Time and Purpose of the Judgment (Dan. 7:11, 12)—It is important to recognize that the judgment in Daniel 7 occurs while the little horn is active on the earth. At the end of verse 8 Daniel hears the "pompous words" of the little horn. Then his attention shifts to the heavenly judgment scene (verses 9, 10). But after describing the judgment scene, Daniel's attention again gets caught by what the horn declares. The text says "at that time," i.e., while he was beholding the heavenly assize, the little horn's proclamation took place here on earth.

Three passages in Daniel 7 refer specifically to the judgment (verses 9-14; 21, 22; and 26). Since the actions of the little horn clearly intersect and, for a time at least, coincide with the heavenly judgment, this judgment cannot be the final one of Revelation 20. Rather, it must be a preliminary judgment going on in heaven prior to the Second Advent, as Seventh-day Adventists have always taught.

Such an interpretation is not limited to Seventh-day Adventists. The Roman Catholic author F. Düsterwald, for example, wrote: "Without question, the prophet Daniel here describes God's judgment concerning the hostile powers. The judgment ends with the total condemnation of the world empires and the triumph of the cause of God. However, what is described here is not, as many older interpreters (Theodoret and others) have assumed, the general judgment of the world, it is not God's judgment here on earth, rather the place of the judgment is in heaven. The context indicates that it is a preliminary judgment which is later confirmed in the general judgment of the world."[12] The Protestant interpreter T. Robinson saw this judgment sitting during the nineteenth century when he wrote his commentary on Daniel. "As already observed, this is not the general judgment at the termination of Christ's reign on earth, or, as the phrase is commonly understood, the end of the world. It appears rather to be an invisible judgment carried on within the veil and revealed by its effects and the execution of its sentence. As occasioned by the 'great words' of the Little Horn, and followed by the taking away of his dominion, it might seem to have already sat. As, however, the sentence is not yet by any means fully executed, it may be sitting now."[13]

What is the purpose of this judgment in Daniel 7? We observe books opened and studied (verse 10). In the Old Testament we find references to the "book of the living" (e.g., Ps. 69:28), the "book of remembrance" (e.g., Mal. 3:16), and to God's "book" (e.g., Ex. 32:32; Ps. 56:8). The same thought occurs in the literature of later Judaism and in the New Testament (e.g., 1 Enoch 47:3; Phil. 4:3; Rev. 3:5; 20:12; 21:27). The important question is Who is being judged from these books? From the context we conclude that this judgment includes:

1. *God's people.* Since "a judgment was made in favor of the saints of the Most High" (Dan. 7:22), they must be in some way the subject of the hearing—a fact not recognized outside of the Seventh-day Adventist Church, though it should not surprise us. Because most Christians believe in the immortality of the soul, they assume that a person's future state gets decided the moment he or she dies. A pre-Advent judgment, therefore, that renders a final decision involving whether a person is saved or not does not fit into their paradigm. They see the dead already in heaven or hell (or purgatory for Roman Catholics). Thus Christians, by and large, have no room for a pre-Advent judgment, though the context in Daniel 7 clearly demands it.

2. *The little horn.* Since the context of the judgment scene repeatedly refers to the little horn (verses 8 and 11), the judgment, therefore, must somehow also involve it. "Internal contextual evidence suggests that the saints and the little horn equally share in the pre-Advent judgment verdict."[14] The saints in the sense that they receive the kingdom (verse 27), and the little horn in that it has its dominion taken away from it. Thus the vindication of the saints (verse 22) implies the condemnation of the little horn.

While non-Adventist interpreters, such as Düsterwald and Robinson, have seen a pre-Advent judgment in Daniel 7, they have limited it to a judgment on the little horn, whereas Seventh-day Adventists have seen both the saints and the little horn as its subjects.

The primary purpose of the investigative pre-Advent judgment is the final confirmation of salvation and vindication of God's people (verse 22). But beyond the vindication of the saints and the condemnation of the little horn, the pre-Advent judgment also corroborates God's justice in His dealings with humanity. When the unfallen beings in the universe examine the records of the saints during the pre-Advent judgment, they will conclude that God has indeed been just and merciful in each case. In this way the character of God, which has been at the center of the great controversy between Christ and Satan, will be exonerated.

The Son of Man Receives the Kingdom (Dan. 7:13, 14)—Many interpreters of Daniel view the coming of the Son of man with the clouds of heaven as a reference to the second advent of Christ.[15] The scene here described, however, does not refer to the Second Advent, since the Ancient of Days is not on earth but in heaven. "He comes to the Ancient of Days in heaven to receive dominion and glory and a kingdom, which will be given Him at the close of His work as a mediator. It is this coming, and not His second advent to the earth, that was foretold in prophecy to take place at the termination of the 2300 days in 1844."[16]

Application

"It is appointed for men to die once, but after this the judgment" (Heb. 9:27). Just as death is the lot of all humanity, so every human being has to face the final judgment, "for we must all appear before the judgment seat of Christ" (2 Cor. 5:10). Although we are saved by faith in Christ (Eph. 2:8), we are still judged by our works (Eccl. 12:14; Matt. 12:36). However, if we have accepted Christ as our Lord and Savior, we have nothing to fear in the judgment because Jesus has taken our sins to the cross and died in our place. Paul says that He was made "sin for us, that we might become the righteousness of God in Him" (2 Cor. 5:21), and that "there is therefore now no condemnation to those who are in Christ Jesus" (Rom. 8:1).

Zechariah 3 graphically demonstrates this wonderful truth. When Satan opposed Joshua before the Lord, God said to His helpers, "Take away the filthy garments from him." Then Joshua received new clothes and a clean turban (verses 4, 5). The filthy garments, representing the sins of the individuals, were not burned or sent to the dry cleaners, but Jesus put them on and then went to the cross to pay the penalty (Rom. 5:8).

The pre-Advent judgment in Daniel 7 is the first phase of the final judgment. It will investigate and decide the cases of "all who have ever entered the service of God."[17] Then at the Second Coming God will reveal the decisions reached in the pre-Advent judgment, and His saints will receive the kingdom (Dan. 7:27). During the millennium the righteous will judge the wicked (Rev. 20:4; 1 Cor. 6:2, 3), and after it the wicked and Satan with all his followers will receive the ultimate penalty—eternal death (Rev. 20:11-15). Together these various phases of judgment constitute the final judgment, the climax of which will be the vindication God's love and righteousness for all eternity.

[1] LeRoy Edwin Froom, *Movement of Destiny* (Washington, D.C.: Review and Herald Pub. Assn., 1971), p. 541.

[2] Walter R. Martin, *The Truth About Seventh-day Adventism* (Grand Rapids: Zondervan, 1960), p. 182.

[3] A. Lacocque, *The Book of Daniel,* pp. 133, 134. On the various interpretations concerning the identity of the "Son of Man" see Arthur J. Ferch, *The Son of Man in Daniel 7,* Andrews University Seminary Doctoral Dissertation Series (Berrien Springs, Mich.: Andrews University Press, 1979), p. 95, n. 2.

[4] J. Montgomery, *The Book of Daniel,* p. 323.

[5] *Ibid.,* pp. 320, 321.

[6] First Enoch 46:3, 5, in J. Charlesworth, *Old Testament Pseudepigrapha,* p. 34.

[7] D. E. Aune, "Son of Man," *International Standard Bible Encyclopedia* (Grand Rapids: W. B. Eerdmans, 1988), vol. 4, p. 576.

[8] Jacques B. Doukhan, *Secrets of Daniel* (Hagerstown, Md.: Review and Herald Pub. Assn., 2000), p. 112.

[9] For other examples of investigative judgments in the Old Testament, see William H. Shea, *Selected Studies on Prophetic Interpretation,* vol. 1, pp. 1-29; Eric Livingston, "Investigative Judgment—A Scriptural Concept," *Ministry,* April 1992, pp. 12-14.

[10] J. A. Seiss, *The Apocalypse* (Grand Rapids: Zondervan, 1973), p. 181.

[11] Samuele Bacchiocchi, "The Pre-Advent Judgement in the New Testament," *Adventists Affirm,* Fall 1994, pp. 37-44, contains additional examples.

[12] F. Düsterwald, *Die Weltreiche und das Gottesreich* (Freiburg: Herder'sche Verlagsbushandlung, 1890), p. 177.

[13] T. Robinson, *Daniel, A Homiletical Commentary* (New York: Funk and Wagnalls, 1892), vol. 19, p. 139. Similarly, S. P. Tregelles, *Remarks on the Prophetic Visions in the Book of Daniel,* 8th ed. (Chelmsford: Sovereign Grace Advent Testimony, n.d.), pp. 36-38.

[14] Norman Gulley, *Christ Is Coming!* (Hagerstown, Md.: Review and Herald Pub. Assn., 1998), p. 413. See also Arthur J. Ferch, "The Pre-Advent Judgment—Is It Scriptural?" *Australasian Record,* Aug. 28, 1982, pp. 5-7.

[15] Bert H. Hall, "Daniel," *The Wesleyan Bible Commentary* (Grand Rapids: W. B. Eerdmans, 1968), vol. 3, p. 535 ; D. K. Campbell, *Daniel: Decoder of Dreams,* p. 84; W. G. Heslop, *Diamonds From Daniel,* p. 104.

[16] Ellen G. White, *The Great Controversy* (Boise, Idaho: Pacific Press Pub. Assn., 1950), p. 480.

[17] *Ibid.*

CHAPTER 9

The Sanctuary Attacked

In chapters 2 and 7 God gave Daniel two glimpses into the future. Then in Daniel 8 the Lord grants him a third one. We saw parallels between the four metal empires of Nebuchadnezzar's vision and the four beasts in Daniel's vision. Furthermore, Daniel 7 added significant new material to the outline of history in chapter 2, such as the rise and the activities of the little horn. The vision of chapter 8 again has considerable overlap with the previous visions, but it also contains a good deal of additional information. The story becomes more and more detailed. The main player in the vision of Daniel 8 is again the little horn. Seven out of 27 verses concern its activities.

With Daniel 7:28 the Aramaic section in the book of Daniel finishes, and in chapter 8 the prophet resumes in Hebrew. Even the symbols employed are different from those in the Aramaic section. Now we have no wild beasts, but the sacrificial creatures of the sanctuary.

Information

The Daily (Heb. Tamîd)—The Hebrew word *tamîd* occurs 104 times in the Old Testament, and the King James Version translates it "daily." Used as an adjective or an adverb, it has the meaning of "continual" or "perpetual." *Tamîd* most often appears in connection with the tabernacle service, in which it can refer to the daily morning and evening burnt offering (Ex. 29:38, 42), the lamp never extinguished (Ex. 27:20), the showbread always on the table (Ex. 25:30), or the fire upon the altar never allowed to go out (Lev. 6:13), etc. "In all instances *tamîd* denotes aspects of the tabernacle or Temple service that were in operation 'continually,' 'regularly,' or 'daily,' in contradistinction to special ritual performed only at specified seasons—such as the Passover, or the Day of Atonement. . . . The 'daily' or 'continual' service represented God's continuing beneficent provision for man, and pointed forward symbolically to Christ's ministry—Christ, who 'ever liveth to make intercession for' us (Heb 7:25)."[1]

The Little Horn—Most modern Bible scholars interpret the little horn in Daniel 7 and 8 as the Syrian king Antiochus IV Epiphanes (175-163 B.C.). In 168 B.C., after a successful campaign against Egypt, Antiochus IV returned home via Judea and encountered an insurrection in progress. He put down the rebellion by massacring thousands of Jewish men, women, and children (2 Macc. 5:12-14). A year later he invaded Egypt again. This time, however, he underwent a humiliating experience when during his march on Alexandria the Roman legate G. Popilius Laenas handed him a letter from the Roman Senate ordering him to leave Egypt. To add insult to injury, Popilius Laenas arrogantly drew a circle around Antiochus and demanded that he respond before stepping outside the circle. Knowing the might of Rome, Antiochus had to acquiesce. He then vented his anger on the Jews. Attempting to make Palestine a Syrian province, he tried to compel the Jews "to abandon their ancestral customs and live no longer by the laws of God" (2 Macc. 6:1). If they did not reject their heritage they would face death. Then he desecrated the Temple in Jerusalem by dedicating it to Olympian Zeus and sacrificing unclean animals on its altar (verses 1-5). His persecution of the Jews led to the Maccabean revolt and the eventual rededication of the Temple on the twenty-fifth of Chislev (December), 164 B.C.

Seventh-day Adventists identify the little horn in Daniel 8 as pagan and papal Rome. They reject the equation of the little horn with Antiochus IV for several reasons: 1. The little horn came up among 10 horns (Dan. 7:8), but Antiochus IV did not emerge among 10 Hellenistic kings. He was the eighth king in the Seleucid kingdom, which had 28 kings during its existence. 2. The vision in Daniel has three horns plucked up before it (verse 8). Antiochus IV did not uproot three kings. 3. The little horn became greater than the other horns (verse 20). Clearly Antiochus IV was not greater than the other kings of his time. In fact, the presence of the Roman ambassador Popilius Laenas was sufficient to cause Antiochus IV to withdraw from Egypt. 4. The saints were given into his hands for three and a half times/years (verse 25). According to 1 Maccabees 1:57 and 4:52-54, the desecration of the Temple lasted only three years and 10 days. 5. The ram (Persia) became great (Dan. 8:4); the goat (Greece) grew very great (verse 8); and the little horn grew exceedingly great (verse 9). At no time was Antiochus IV greater than Medo-Persia or Greece.

A study of the little horns in Daniel 7 and 8 indicates a strong parallelism between them: 1. Both horns are little in the beginning (Dan. 7:8; 8:9). 2. Both become great later on (Dan. 7:20; 8:9ff.). 3. Both are persecuting powers (Dan. 7:21, 25; 8:10, 24). 4. Both are self-exalting and blasphemous (Dan. 7:8, 20, 25; 8:10, 11, 25). 5. Both target God's people (Dan. 7:25; 8:24). 6. Both have aspects of their activity delineated by prophetic time (Dan. 7:25; 8:13, 14). 7. Both extend until the time of the end (Dan. 7:25, 26; 8:17, 19). 8. And both face supernatural destruction (Dan. 7:11, 26; 8:25).

Since in Daniel 7 the little-horn symbolism clearly points to the Papacy, the little horn in Daniel 8 must refer to the same power. The only difference between the two chapters is that in Daniel 8 the little horn symbolizes pagan Rome (Dan. 8:9, 10) as well as papal Rome (verses 11, 12).

Explanation

The vision in Daniel 8:1-14 is the climax of the symbolic presentations in the book. What follows from Daniel 8:15 to the end of the book is supplementary to the vision of chapter 8. The end of chapter 8 tells us that Daniel did not understand (verse 27). In chapter 9, therefore, Daniel seeks further understanding (verse 3), and the visiting angel admonishes him to "understand the vision," saying, "I have now come forth to give you skill to understand" (see verses 22-25).

The Ram and the Goat (Dan 8:1-8)—In 548/547B.C.[2] Daniel is in a vision transported to Susa, the city that, after the collapse of Babylon, would become the capital of the Persian Empire. At the canal called Ulai he watches a goat defeating a ram. Verse 20 explains the symbolism—the ram represents Medo-Persia and the goat the Greek kingdom of Alexander, who is the notable horn between the eyes of the goat (verse 5). At the height of the goat's strength the big horn breaks, and four other horns appear in its place. Commentators generally agree that the four horns represent the four divisions of the Greek kingdom after the death of Alexander the Great.[3]

The Origin of the Little Horn (Dan. 8:9)—Most commentators assume that the little horn came out of one of the four horns, but contextual and literary-structural grounds make that unlikely.[4] The previous verse ended with the words "In place of it [the notable horn] four notable ones came up toward the four winds of heaven." The immediate antecedent of "one of them," therefore, is "the four winds of heaven," not the four horns. The geographical expansion of the little horn (south, east, beautiful land) suggests that its emergence also belongs to the geographical plane, i.e., it comes out of one of the four points of the compass. Furthermore, the verb *yatza,* used for the "coming out" of the little horn (verse 9), stands in contrast to the verb *'alah,* used for the "coming up" of the other horns (verses 3 and 8).

The non-Adventist author A. Bloomfield also recognizes that the little horn emerges from one of the four winds. "The little horn, we are told, is to come out of one of the four winds of heaven (verse 8). Which wind it is, is immediately indicated: he will wax great toward the south, east, and toward Palestine."[5] Hence it must originate either from the north or the west. The power that followed the Greek kingdoms in the east and south was Rome, and it emerged from the west. The Seleucid Empire became a Roman province around 65 B.C., Palestine became incorporated into the Roman Empire in 63 B.C., and Rome took over Egypt in 30 B.C.

But where is the beast to which the horn belongs? One possibility is that it is outside of the frame of the vision, and thus Daniel does not see it. The reason for this could be that the animals symbolizing Medo-Persia and Greece in Daniel 8 were ritually clean ones, while any "terrible beast," such as used to symbolize Rome in Daniel 7, would have been an unclean creature. "That would have distorted the connection between the vision and the sanctuary."[6] However, in biblical symbolism horns represent powers or nations, and they can appear by themselves without the animals to which they naturally belong. Zechariah 1:18, 19, for example, tells how the prophet sees four horns by themselves, and an angel explains that "these are the horns [nations] that have scattered Judah, Israel, and Jerusalem" (verse 19).

In contrast to Daniel 7, in which the little horn (papal Rome) emerges from the fourth beast (pagan Rome), in Daniel 8 the little horn symbolizes both pagan and papal Rome. "A part of the whole (the horn) symbolizes the whole (the fourth beast of Daniel 7). We find support for this conclusion in the fact that in Daniel 8 the little horn participates in a *horizontal* conquest—it goes against the south (Egypt), the east (Syria), and the Beautiful Land (Israel)—representing the activity of *pagan* Rome (Dan. 8:9). But it also reaches up to heaven (a *vertical* expansion against the people of God and the role of the Prince in the heavenly temple)—the work of *papal* Rome (verses 10-12). This horn incorporates the activity of the beast and its horn described in Daniel 7."[7]

The parallelism between the prophecies in Daniel 2, 7, and 8 helps us to understand the symbolism of the little horn in Daniel 8.

Symbol	Daniel 2	Daniel 7	Daniel 8
Babylon	Head of gold	Lion	——
Medo-Persia	Chest and arms of silver	Bear	Ram
Greece	Belly and thighs of bronze	Leopard	Goat
Rome	Legs of iron	Dreadful beast	Little horn (pagan and papal Rome).
Divided Europe	Feet of iron and clay	10 horns	It warred against Christ, cast down the sanctuary, and continued to the time of the end
Papacy	——	Little horn	
Second Advent	Stone cut without hands	Saints receive kingdom	

The Activities of the Little Horn (Dan. 8:9-12; 23-25)—Having established the origin and identity of the little horn, we can turn our attention to its activities: 1. It cast down some of the host and some of the stars to the ground. 2. It exalted itself as high as the Prince of the host. 3. It took away the daily and cast down the place of God's sanctuary. 4. It cast truth to the ground.

1. *It cast down some of the host and some of the stars to the ground* (Dan. 8:10, 24).—Exodus 12:41 describes the hosts of the Lord as Israel. In Daniel's vision the "host of heaven" refers to God's people who are still here on earth but have their citizenship in heaven (Phil. 3:20). Thus one can interpret the host of heaven in Daniel 8:24 as indicating the holy people, and the stars most likely represent the leaders of the host (see Rev. 1:20).

The Roman emperors persecuted the Jews as well as the Christians. When Rome destroyed Jerusalem and its Temple in A.D. 70, more than 1 million Jews perished.[8] And during the first two centuries of the Christian Era the emperors Nero, Decius, and Diocletian murdered thousands of Christians who refused to offer incense to the emperor. The church historian Eusebius (fourth century) tells us, "One cannot but admire those who suffered also in their native land where thousands of men, women, and children, despising the present life for the sake of our Savior's doctrine, submitted to death in various shapes. Some, after being tortured with scrapings, the rack, the most dreadful scourgings, and other innumerable agonies which one might shudder to hear, were finally committed to the flames. Some plunged and drowned in the sea, others voluntarily offered their own heads to the executioners, others died in the midst of their torments, some wasted away by famine, and others were fixed to the cross. Some, indeed, were executed as malefactors usually were; others, more cruelly, were nailed with the head downwards and kept alive until they were destroyed by starving on the cross itself."[9]

   2. *It exalted itself as high as the Prince of the host* (Dan. 8:11, 25).—Verses 9 and 10 depicted the movements of the little horn on a horizontal plane, while verses 11 and 12 show a vertical dimension, indicating the change of activities from pagan Rome to papal Rome.[10]

   In Joshua the commander of the Lord's army is a divine being (Joshua 5:14, 15). The Prince of the host of God's people must be the one called "Messiah the Prince" in Daniel 9:25, "Michael, your prince" in Daniel 10:21, and "Michael, . . . the great prince who stands watch over the sons of your people" in Daniel 12:1, i.e., Christ.

   How did the little horn magnify itself against Christ? By openly assuming the office of Christ as mediator between God and humanity, the Papacy exalted itself against the Prince of the host and fulfilled 2 Thessalonians 2:4.

   3. *It took away the daily and cast down the place of God's sanctuary* (Dan. 8:11).—How did the Papacy remove the daily sacrifice and cast down the place of His sanctuary? By placing human intercession into the hands of priests, the use of the confessional, and by sacrificing Christ anew in every Mass, the Papacy has eclipsed Christ's heavenly ministry in the minds of the worshipers. Believers no longer approach Christ directly; instead they go to the priest, to the saints, or to Mary. By substituting the priest's service here on earth for Christ's role in the heavenly sanctuary the little horn has symbolically "cast down the place of his sanctuary" to the earth and thereby defiled it.

   In the sacrifice of the Mass the Roman priest becomes an *alter Christus,* that is, "another Christ," in that he sacrifices the real Christ upon the altar and presents Him for the salvation of the faithful. We see this clearly taught in the latest edition (1994) of the *Catechism* of the Roman Catholic Church. "The sacrifice of Christ and the sacrifice of the Eucharist [Mass] are *one single sacrifice:* 'The victim is one and the same: the same now offers through the ministry of priests, who then offered himself on the cross; only the manner of offering is different.' 'In this divine sacrifice which is celebrated in the Mass, the same Christ who offered himself once in a bloody manner on the altar of the cross is contained and is offered in an unbloody manner." [11]

Furthermore, the priest changes the substance of bread and wine into the true substance of Christ's body and blood. "The bread and wine are brought to the altar; they will be offered by the priest in the name of Christ in the Eucharistic sacrifice in which they will become his body and blood." [12] In other words, in obedience to the priest's words Christ descends on the altar in every Mass. The Jesuit priest Franz Xaver Esser wrote: "Oh priest, how superhuman and great you are, you are like Christ who commanded the wind and the sea, and who walked on the heaving waves. . . . With his scepter the priest enters heaven and takes the Son of God from the closed circle of the angelic choir and they all are powerless, they cannot prevent it." [13]

In the confessional the priest forgives sins by the formula "I absolve you from your sins in the name of the Father, the Son, and the Holy Spirit." It is a miraculous key in the hands of the priest. Says the *Catechism,* "Bishops and priests, by virtue of the sacrament of Holy Orders, have the power to forgive all sins 'in the name of the Father, and of the Son, and of the Holy Spirit.'" [14]

It is through such teaching that the ministry of Christ in the heavenly sanctuary has been overthrown in the minds of many Christians and its place effectively taken by misleading substitutes. The Mass and the confessional draw the minds of Christian believers away from a continual dependence upon the mediatorial ministry of the Savior in His sanctuary. Elaborate ceremonies, all in the name of Christ, obscure the ministry of Christ. "Instead of trust in the inspired Word and in the personal ministry of the Holy Spirit men are taught to depend upon an infallible church and an authoritative teaching body, and so to receive such false doctrines as transsubstantiation, purgatory, adoration of images, immortality of the soul, the sacrifice of the Mass, the immaculate conception. Our great High Priest, who invites us to come to His throne of grace and find grace to help in time of need, finds His perpetual intercession pushed aside, and other means of grace, other mediators and intercessors, are interposed between Him and His people. . . . His place is taken in the Roman system by human priests who offer sacrifices, forgive sins, and confer the Holy Spirit.

81

The church is born on the shoulders of the pope and upon the heart of Mary instead of upon the shoulders and heart of Christ. Most of these false principles have grown stronger through the centuries, but none of them can be traced even in primitive form to a date much before the fifth century A.D."[15]

4. *It cast truth to the ground* (Dan. 8:12).—Jesus said of Himself, "I am . . . the truth" (John 14:6), and in regard to God's Word, He said, "Your Word is truth" (John 17:17). From the twelfth century onward various popes prohibited the use of the Bible in the vernacular because the Waldenses and later the Protestants used it against the teachings of the church.

The Council of Trent in 1546 decreed that no one was to interpret Scripture contrary to the opinion of the church, for the church was the judge of the true sense of Scripture. "No one, relying on his own skill, shall—in matters of faith, and of morals pertaining to the edification of Christian doctrine—wresting the sacred Scripture to his own senses, presume to interpret the said sacred Scripture contrary to that sense which holy mother Church—whose it is to judge of the true sense and interpretation of the holy Scriptures—hath held and doth hold; or even contrary to the unanimous consent of the Fathers."[16]

Today, of course, the picture has changed. In 1943 Pope Pius XII issued an encyclical urging priests to study and preach from Scripture, to help Catholic associations for the spread of Scripture in modern languages, and to encourage the laity to read the Bible daily.[17] However, it does not mean that the Bible is now the absolute norm of faith for the Catholic Church today. The Second Vatican Council (1962-1965) declared that "she [the church] has always regarded, and continues to regard, the Scriptures, taken together with sacred Tradition, as the supreme rule of her faith," and "sacred theology relies on the written Word of God, taken together with sacred Tradition, as on a permanent foundation."[18] Thus while the leadership encourages Bible reading, Roman Catholics accept tradition as being on an equal level with Scripture.

Application

When speaking of the little horn, we must distinguish between the institution of the Papacy and the people who support or follow its teaching. The members in the Roman Catholic Church, including the pope, are people for whom Christ died. Throughout history countless sincere and devout Christians have been members of the Roman Catholic Church. Ellen White wrote that "there are true Christians in every church who do not know the origin of the Sunday-sabbath, and believe that they are keeping the day which God sanctified and blest. This is true of worshipers even in the Catholic Church; and while this ignorance and integrity remain, God accepts of their sincerity; but when light shall fall upon their pathway, God requires them to come into harmony with his law, and to observe the Sabbath of His appointing."[19]

Like Luther, Zwingli, and Calvin in the time of the Reformation, God's people in all Christian churches at the time of the end will hear the voice of the fourth angel in Revelation 18 calling, "Come out of her, my people," and they will respond by joining themselves to God's remnant people. In our written and spoken witness, therefore, we need to be careful that we do not unnecessarily offend people. Again Ellen White has given us wise counsel: "In bearing the message make no personal thrusts at other churches, not even the Roman Catholic Church. In the different denominations angels of God see many who can be reached only by the greatest caution. Therefore let us be careful of our words."[20] While we must never compromise the truth, we should always be mindful of the fact that others are nevertheless people for whom Christ died and whom He loves.

---

[1] *Seventh-day Adventist Bible Dictionary,* pp. 257, 258.

[2] G. F. Hasel, "The First and Third Years of Belshazzar (Dan 7:1; 8:1)," *Andrews University Seminary Studies* 15 (1977): 153-168.

[3] See comments on Daniel 7:1-7.

[4] See Martin Pröbstle, "A Text-Oriented Study of Daniel 8:9-14" (unpublished Ph.D. dissertation, Andrews University, 2003), pp. 100-105.

[5] Arthur E. Bloomfield, *The End of the Days* (Minneapolis: Bethany Fellowship, 1961), p. 165.

[6] Angel Rodríguez, *Future Glory* (Hagerstown, Md.: Review and Herald Pub. Assn., 2002), p. 50.

[7] *Ibid.* In contrast to Rodríguez, I see the activities of pagan Rome in verses 9 and 10, not only in verse 9.

[8] Josephus *Wars of the Jews* 6. 9. 3.

[9] *Eusebius' Ecclesiastical History* 8. 8. 1, trans. C. F. Cruse (Peabody, Mass.: Hendrickson, 1998), pp. 287, 288.

[10] Gerhard F. Hasel, "The 'Little Horn,' the Heavenly Sanctuary, and the Time of the End: A Study of Daniel 8:9-14," *Symposium on Daniel,* ed. Frank B. Holbrook (Washington, D.C.: Biblical Research Institute, 1986), vol. 2, p. 401.

[11] *Catechism of the Catholic Church* (Mahwah, N.J.: Paulist Press, 1994), no. 1367.

[12] *Ibid.,* no. 1350.

[13] Franz Xaver Esser, *Zepter und Schlüssel in der Hand des Priesters* (Freiburg im Breisgau: Herder and Co., 1924), p. 15.

[14] *Catechism of the Catholic Church,* no. 1461.

[15] Ernest W. Marter, *Daniel's Philosophy of History* (Bracknell, Eng.: Newbold College, 1967), pp. 78, 79.

[16] Philip Schaff, *The Creeds of Christendom,* 4th ed. (New York: Harper, 1919), vol. 2,

p. 83.

[17] *Divino Afflante Spiritu,* Sept. 30, 1943, in D. F. Neufeld, ed., *Seventh-day Adventist Bible Students' Source Book,* pp. 155, 156.

[18] Austin P. Flannery, *Documents of Vatican II* (Grand Rapids: W. B. Eerdmans, 1975), pp. 762, 763.

[19] Ellen G. White, in *Signs of the Times,* Nov. 19, 1894.

[20] White, in *Pacific Union Recorder,* Oct. 23, 1902.

CHAPTER 10

The Sanctuary Cleansed

Seventh-day Adventists believe that Daniel 8:9-14 refers to the great controversy or spiritual conflict between Christ and Satan. In particular it concerns the contrast between God's plan of salvation and the counterfeit system of the little horn. This passage is at the heart of the prophetic messages of Daniel as well as at the center of the Adventist sanctuary doctrine. A correct understanding of the texts, therefore, is important for a proper perspective of the sanctuary message and the three angels' messages, the first of which proclaims that "the hour of His judgment has come" (Rev. 14:7).

Information

The Old Testament Sanctuary Service—While the Israelites camped at Mount Sinai after their deliverance from Egypt, God instructed Moses to build Him a sanctuary (Ex. 25:8, 9) and to establish a service that would serve as a visible illustration of the plan of salvation. The sanctuary itself, surrounded by a large courtyard, consisted of two rooms, the holy and the Most Holy, corresponding to the two phases of ministry—the daily and the yearly service. The daily service took place in the courtyard and in the holy place, the yearly service in the Most Holy Place.

The daily service consisted of the regular morning and evening burnt offerings and the offerings the Israelites brought throughout the day. All of them pointed to Christ, the Lamb of God (John 1:29). The most important offering was the sin offering. According to Leviticus 4:2, 13, 22, 27, however, sin offerings were only for acts done through ignorance. People might commit a sin and not know it (Lev. 4:13; 5:2-4). But when they discovered it, they were to bring an offering. In cases of conscious or presumptuous sins, in Hebrew called "sins done with a high hand," the offender was to die (Num. 15:30, 31; Deut. 22:22). This happened to the man found gathering sticks on the Sabbath (Num. 15:35, 36).

It did not mean, however, that a person could not have such sins forgiven. Sins, however heinous, could be and were forgiven, as they are now, by repentance and restitution, as happened in the case of David's adultery and murder (Ps. 51:16, 17). People in such cases received forgiveness, not because of a sacrifice the offender brought, but in view of the cross of Christ. It would have cheapened the enormity of sin and humanity's conception of the holiness of God if the man in Numbers 15 had been permitted to bring an ox or a lamb for a deliberate transgression of one of the 10 commandments. Therefore it was "not possible that the blood of bulls and goats could take away sins" (Heb. 10:4). Such offerings were only illustrations of the real sacrifice of Christ. Only the death of our Lord on the cross provides for the removal of sin. "But now, once at the end of the ages, He has appeared to put away sin by the sacrifice of Himself" (Heb. 9:26). The expression "once" or "once for all," in connection with the sacrifice of Christ, is deeply significant. "Christ . . . suffered *once* for sins" (1 Peter 3:18); "Christ was offered *once* to bear the sins of many" (Heb. 9:28); and "now *once* in the end of the world" (verse 26, KJV). Thus the Catholic doctrine that Christ is sacrificed for our sins in every Mass is unbiblical.

The offerings symbolically transferred the sins of Israel to the sanctuary, thereby defiling it. As a result, a special service was necessary to cleanse the sanctuary from the sins that had accumulated throughout the year. God commanded that an atonement be made for the sanctuary to "cleanse it, and consecrate it from the uncleanness of the children of Israel" (Lev. 16:19). The special service took place on the Day of Atonement. On that day, once a year, the Levites brought two young goats to the sanctuary and the high priest cast lots upon them, "one lot for the Lord and the other lot for the scapegoat" (verse 8). The priest slew the goat of the Lord as a sin offering, and the high priest took its blood into the Most Holy and sprinkled it on and before the mercy seat. The ritual made atonement for the sanctuary and cleansed it from the sins of the people. When the high priest had finished making the atonement for the sanctuary, he placed his hands on the scapegoat and confessed over it all the iniquities of the children of Israel and sent it by the hand of a man into the wilderness and allowed it to escape (hence the name "scapegoat").

It is important to remember that the scapegoat was not slain; therefore, we cannot consider it an atonement for sin, for without the shedding of blood there is no remission of sin (Heb. 9:22). The scapegoat symbolized Satan, who must ultimately bear the responsibility not only for his own sins but for his part in all the sins he has caused others to commit. "While the sin offering pointed to Christ as a sacrifice, and the high priest represented Christ as a mediator, the scapegoat typified Satan, the author of sin, upon whom the sins of the truly penitent will finally be placed. When the high priest, by virtue of the blood of the sin offering, removed the sins from the sanctuary, he placed them upon the scapegoat. When Christ, by virtue of His own blood, removes the sins of His people from the heavenly sanctuary at the close of His ministration, He will place them upon Satan, who, in the execution of the judgment, must bear the final penalty."[1]

In cases in which the defilement of the Temple resulted from desecration by God's enemies or the people's idolatry, the Temple was also cleansed, restored, and sanctified. For example, when Hezekiah came to the throne, one of the first actions he took was to sanctify or reconsecrate the Temple that his father, Ahaz, had desecrated (2 Chron. 29:3-8). In the process, the priests went into the inner part of the Temple "to cleanse [taher] it, and brought out all the debris that they found in the temple of the Lord" (verse 16). The Hebrew word taher, used here for the physical cleansing of the Temple, is the same word employed in Leviticus 16:30 for the spiritual or ritual purification of the Temple from sin.

Explanation

In the previous chapter we saw that the little horn in Daniel 8, which we identified as pagan and papal Rome, persecuted God's people, usurped Christ's ministry of intercession, and cast the foundation of Christ's sanctuary and His truth to the ground.

The Conversation (Dan. 8:13, 14)—Having observed the activities of the little horn, Daniel then hears two heavenly beings speaking with each other. One asks the other, "How long will the vision be, concerning the daily sacrifices and the transgression of desolation, the giving of both the sanctuary and the host to be trampled underfoot?" And the other being replies, "For two thousand three hundred days; then the sanctuary shall be cleansed" (Dan. 8:13, 14). Some have made the mistake of limiting the question and its answer to the activities of the little horn. They interpret the time period of 2300 days as referring only to the devastation caused by the little-horn power. But the question applies to the whole vision, which began in the time of the Persians, symbolized by the ram at its beginning (verse 3). Literally the question begins with the words "Until when the vision?" Although the question lists some of the terrible activities of the little horn, things that obviously shocked the prophet, *"the question is not*

How long will this activity continue?

about how long the little horn is going to profane the sanctuary but about when the content of the whole vision will be fulfilled. The answer indicates that the fulfillment of the *whole vision* will take 2300 days/years. At the end of this period the little horn's usurpation of the priestly work of the Messiah will come to an end through the eschatological day of atonement."[2] In the next chapter we will see why Adventists understand 1844 to be the ending of the 2300 days/years and the beginning of the pre-Advent judgment.

The prophecy of Daniel 8 focuses on the religious conflict between the Prince of the host and the little horn. In this conflict "there have been two rival plans of sanctuary ministry and salvation—the heavenly original and the earthly substitute. There have been two rival sanctuaries and two rival priesthoods. There have been two rival high priests who have officiated over these plans. At some point in the history of this struggle, there must come a time for a decision between these two plans and their results. There has to come a time of judgment that will decide between them. This judgment is what is brought to view in the time period of Daniel 8:14, the 2300 days."[3] At the end of the 2300 days a final decision will determine which of the two plans has been the true plan of salvation. This involves an examination of the nature of each plan and their effects upon their respective recipients. The pre-Advent investigative judgment described in Daniel 7:9-14 is chronologically located at the end of the 2300 prophetic days.

The pre-Advent investigation examines the records of the lives of the believers. At its conclusion it blots out either their sins or their names from the heavenly record. Through this pre-Advent judgment the true plan of salvation is established and the scheme of the little horn is condemned. The spiritual conflict between the two systems is decided, and God is justified before the universe (Rom. 3:4). In other words, the pre-Advent judgment vindicates not only the saints but also God before all created beings, including Satan and his followers.

Because tradition had obscured the truth about Christ's ministry in heaven and Protestantism had only partly recovered it, neither William Miller nor any contemporary scholar understood clearly which sanctuary Daniel 8:14 referred to. In the years following 1844, however, Bible students gave special study to the books of Exodus and Leviticus in connection with the book of Hebrews, and the distinction between the "continual" ministration of Christ in the heavenly temple since His ascension and the "final" or "closing" ministration that He performs immediately prior to His second advent began to be understood.

"Since that time the doctrine of the sanctuary has been put right, the truth thrown down has been lifted up, and for those who have been privileged to learn of these things, Jesus their Prince is no longer a Sacrifice only, but also a merciful and faithful High Priest, and more, He has entered upon His final work and soon all enemies will be under His feet."[4]

The Day of Atonement—The cleansing of the heavenly sanctuary from the sins of the faithful corresponds to the cleansing of the Mosaic tabernacle on the Day of Atonement (Lev. 16:30).

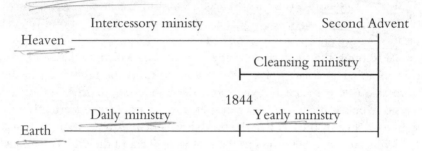

It is important to remember that on the Day of Atonement the morning and evening sacrifices continued (Num. 28:3, 4), just as Christ continues His intercessory ministry since 1844 (Heb. 7:25); otherwise, nobody's sins could today be forgiven. However, since 1844 Christ in addition to the ministry of intercession is performing a ministry of cleansing—the pre-Advent judgment.

The primary objective of the pre-Advent judgment or cleansing of the heavenly sanctuary is the blotting out of the sins of the saints, but this is not all. According to the context in Daniel 8 not only do the books of heaven need to be cleansed, but God also must address the havoc caused by the attacks of the little horn (verses 11, 12).

That which was symbolically cast down—the daily sacrifice, the truth, and the place of His sanctuary—will be restored figuratively at the end of the 2300 years. How has God accomplished this restoration since 1844? First, by reversing earthly judgments against the saints in the heavenly court. Second, through the proclamation of Christ's high-priestly ministry in heaven in the first angel's message (Rev. 14:7).

Thus Daniel 8:14 teaches two vital truths: (a) that since 1844 the sanctuary is being cleansed from the record of the sins of God's people that have been transferred there as faithful believers have, down through the ages, laid their sins upon Jesus, their sin-bearer, representative, and substitutionary priest, and (b) that since 1844 the sanctuary has been restored to its rightful place through the proclamation of the first angel's message.

Cleansing the Sanctuary—Many modern Bibles do not use the word "cleansed" in Daniel 8:14. Rather they speak of a restoration or re-consecration of the sanctuary. For example, the Revised Standard Version translates the passage as "the sanctuary shall be restored to its rightful state." The Hebrew word *nitsdaq,* used only here in the whole Old Testament, is a passive form of the common Old Testament word *tsadaq,* meaning "to be just or righteous, to be in the right," and in the passive form "to be made right, to be justified." Hence, in its root meaning it allows for the idea of being "put right" or "restored."

"Although the modern renderings of *nitsdaq,* which are based on the root meaning of *tsadaq,* serve well to convey to us the restoration of the truth about the sanctuary, yet the older rendering in the Authorized Version, 'be cleansed,' conveys a deeper truth. This older rendering is fully supported, first by the fact that the pre-Christian Greek translations of *tsadaq* (which occurs over 500 times in the Masoretic Text of the Old Testament) reveal that the word was understood to have a very wide range of meaning, of which 'to cleanse' is one. In harmony with this, both the LXX and Theodotion translate *nitsdaq* by *katharizo,* 'to cleanse' in Dan 8:14 (J. P. Justesen, in *Andrews University Seminary Studies* IV [1964]: 53-61)."[5]

Critics have sometimes accused Seventh-day Adventists of basing their sanctuary doctrine on a faulty translation of Daniel 8:14 in the King James Version. However, a survey of ancient and modern Bible versions shows that a number of other versions besides the KJV translate *nitsdaq* as "cleansed." It is particularly interesting to note that the latest translation of the Jewish Publication Society (1988) again translates *nitsdaq* as "cleansed."

LXX	"the sanctuary shall be cleansed"
Theodotion	"the sanctuary shall be cleansed"
KJV	"the sanctuary shall be cleansed"
NKJV	"the sanctuary shall be cleansed"
RSV	"the sanctuary shall be restored to its rightful state"
NEB	"the Holy Place shall emerge victorious"
NIV	"the sanctuary will be reconsecrated"
NASB	"the holy place will be properly restored"
Douay	"the sanctuary shall be cleansed"
Knox	"the sanctuary is cleansed"
Jerusalem	"the sanctuary shall have its rights restored"

Moffatt	"the sanctuary shall be restored"
MT	"the sanctuary shall be victorious"
Tanakh	"the sanctuary shall be cleansed"

Thus the KJV translation "the sanctuary shall be cleansed" is linguistically, contextually, and historically well justified.

The diagram on page 92 shows that the cleansing of the sanctuary in Daniel 8 is the same event as the pre-Advent judgment in Daniel 7. In Daniel 7 the judgment scene follows the activities of the little horn during the 1260-day period. Daniel 8 has the sanctuary cleansed at the end of the 2300 prophetic days after the little horn has warred against Christ and His sanctuary. And in Daniel 7 the saints are given into the little horn's hands for three and a half times, or 1260 years, i.e., until 1798. Following the activities of the little horn, Daniel sees a judgment taking place in heaven that abolishes the power of the little horn. From Daniel 8 (and 9) we learn that this judgment, which is equivalent to the cleansing of the sanctuary, began in 1844.

Application

The idea of standing in front of a judge unnerves most people. Yet the Bible contains many texts referring to God's judgment. For example: "The ungodly shall not stand in the judgment" (Ps. 1:5); "We must all appear before the judgment seat of Christ" (2 Cor. 5:10); "For God will bring every work into judgment, including every secret thing, whether good or evil" (Eccl. 12:14); "For every idle word men may speak, they will give account of it in the day of judgment" (Matt. 12:36). Are such texts good news for us, or are they unsettling? Does anyone look forward to his or her judgment?

Well, yes, the psalmist actually did eagerly anticipate the judgment. He longed for it. In Psalm 82:8 he prayed, "Arise, O God, judge the earth." When we have been wronged, perhaps we have been tempted to pray, "Arise, O Lord, and judge these evil people." But David not only prayed that God would judge the wicked in our world; numerous times he prayed, "Judge me, O Lord" (Ps. 7:8; 26:1; 35:24; 43:1, KJV). He seemed to be saying, "Hurry up, Lord, judge me." Why? Did he not realize the heinousness of his own sins (adultery and murder)? Yes, David understood: "I acknowledge my transgressions, and my sin is always before me" (Ps. 51:3). But he also grasped the message of righteousness by faith. He recognized that sinful though he was, the blood of the Substitute could cover and cleanse his sins. Therefore, in joy he could cry out, "Blessed is he

91

whose transgression is forgiven, whose sin is covered" (Ps. 32:1).

Scripture consistently upholds the seriousness of sin and the certainty of judgment, but it also reveals repeatedly that the Lamb of God, the sinner's substitute, has been accepted in each person's place (Rom. 3:23-28). As we receive Christ, His righteousness covers us, acquitting, pardoning, and cleansing us, and therefore we need not fear the judgment (Rom. 8:1).

PARALLELS BETWEEN DANIEL 7 AND 8

DEMONSTRATING THE SIGNIFICANT LINK BETWEEN
THE PRE-ADVENT SESSION OF THE JUDGMENT
AND THE "CLEANSING OF THE SANCTUARY"
OF DANIEL 8:14

DANIEL 7	DANIEL 8
LION (BABYLON)	(BABYLON OMITTED)
BEAR (MEDO-PERSIA)	RAM (MEDO-PERSIA)
LEOPARD (GREECE)	HE-GOAT (GREECE)
FOURTH BEAST (PAGAN ROME)	LITTLE HORN (ROME, PAGAN AND PAPAL)
TEN HORNS (10 KINGDOMS)	WARRED AGAINST CHRIST. CAST DOWN SANCTUARY. CONTINUED TO THE "TIME OF THE END."
LITTLE HORN (PAPAL ROME)	
THE NEXT GREAT EVENT? **THE JUDGMENT SITS** THE LITTLE HORN'S DOMINION TAKEN AWAY.	THE NEXT GREAT EVENT? **THE SANCTUARY IS CLEANSED** THE LITTLE HORN "BROKEN WITHOUT HAND."
THE SAINTS OF THE MOST HIGH POSSESS THE KINGDOM.	CHAPTERS 9-12 ARE A CONTINUATION OF GABRIEL'S INTERPRETATION, BEGUN IN CHAPTER 8 AND CLIMAXING IN **THE FINAL DELIVERANCE OF GOD'S PEOPLE.**

Source: Frank Breaden, *New Pictorial Aid* (Warburton, Victoria, Australia: Signs Pub. Co., 1987), p. 55.

The Importance of the Pre-Advent Judgment—In our study of Daniel 7 and 8 we have discovered that (1) the parallels between Daniel 7 and 8 indicate that the judgment in Daniel 7 and the cleansing of the sanctuary in Daniel 8 are one and the same event, and (2) the subjects of the judgment in Daniel 7 are the little horn (verses 8-11) and the saints (verse 22). What is the importance of the doctrine of the pre-Advent judgment?

First, its historical significance lies in the fact that it provides an understanding of the disappointment in 1844. The recognition that Jesus in 1844 began the second phase of His ministry in heaven explains why He did not come to earth on October 22, 1844 (Rev. 10:9, 10).

Second, it is theologically vital in the sense that the pre-Advent judgment serves as the final review for the lives of those who will enter the kingdom. "From time to time some of these saints have been adjudged guilty of various crimes by earthly tribunals when actually they were serving God and man faithfully. In the pre-Advent judgment these unjust sentences by earthly court will be reversed by the courts of heaven. In this way God will vindicate His saints."[6]

Finally, the pre-Advent judgment will proclaim the righteousness, justice, and mercy of God throughout the universe (Rev. 15:3, 4). It will vindicate the character of God, which has been in dispute in His dispute with Satan (Rom. 3:4).

[1] E. G. White, *The Great Controversy*, p. 422.

[2] A. Rodríguez, *Future Glory*, p. 54.

[3] William H. Shea, *Daniel 7-12*, Abundant Life Bible Amplifier (Boise, Idaho: Pacific Press Pub. Assn., 1996), p. 110.

[4] E. W. Marter, *Daniel's Philosophy of History*, p. 82.

[5] *Ibid.*

[6] William H. Shea, "Theological Importance of the Pre-Advent Judgment," in *Seventy Weeks, Leviticus, and the Nature of Prophecy*, ed. Frank B. Holbrook, Daniel and Revelation Committee Series (Washington, D.C.: Biblical Research Institute, 1986), vol. 3, p. 328.

CHAPTER 11

God's Timetable

Approximately 10 years had passed since Daniel had received the vision of the 2300 evenings and mornings recorded in chapter 8. Though an angel told him to "seal up the vision, for it refers to many days in the future" (Dan. 8:26), he longed to know what the long time period of 2300 evenings and mornings meant. According to Jeremiah's prophecy (Jer. 29:10), the time for the return of the Jews to Jerusalem in 539 B.C. was close at hand. Yet in his last vision, the angel had told him that it would be 2300 prophetic days before the sanctuary would be restored. Daniel no doubt feared that God somehow intended to prolong the period of captivity. In response to these concerns the Lord sent Gabriel to assure him that it was not the case. The first 490 years of the 2300, he learned, had special significance for the Jews, for toward the end of the period the promised Messiah would come.

Information

A Covenant Lawsuit—For one to grasp the significance of Stephen's speech in A.D. 34 as the end of the 490-year period, it is important to understand the Old Testament lawsuit concept (Heb. *rîb*). A *rîb* refers to a dispute requiring a judge to adjudicate it. Particularly in the prophetic literature, a *rîb* is a covenant lawsuit between Israel and Yahweh. When the prophets came as reformers to call Israel back to the Sinai covenant relationship, they did so through a "covenant lawsuit," in which the prophet summoned the people to hear the charge Yahweh had against them.

An example of such a covenant lawsuit appears in Micah 6:1-8. Verses 1 and 2, in which *rîb* occurs three times, call upon the mountains to serve as witnesses. With their knowledge of generations of human misdeeds and of God's dealings with Israel, they are summoned to hear Yahweh's charge against His people. Rather than spell out the charge of disloyalty, God asks

94

His people what He has done to them that they abandoned Him. "How have I wearied [burdened] you?" He says. Why have they ceased to obey Him? To show that they had no reason for such behavior, the prophet cites God's mighty acts on behalf of His people in the past (verses 3-5). He delivered them from Egypt and brought them safely through the wilderness to Canaan. His recital reminds us of God's faithfulness to His covenant promise.

In verses 6, 7 Micah now voices the people's response. If Yahweh is displeased with us, what shall we do? they ask. Shall we come to Him with yearling calves—the choicest offering? Or shall we give thousands of rams and rivers of oil—is it quantity that matters? "The series of hypothetical questions rises to a hysterical and ghastly crescendo in the ultimate offer of child sacrifice."[1] The implied answer to all these questions is that God requires none of these things—what is important is not what we have in our hands but what is in our hearts. Sacrifice without a proper relationship to God and one's neighbor is useless. Verse 8 then summarizes the essential elements of God's covenant with Israel—do justly, love mercy, and walk humbly with Him.

The Command to Restore and Build Jerusalem—The angel Gabriel told Daniel that the starting point for the 490-year prophecy was the command to restore and build Jerusalem. The books of Ezra and Nehemiah record four decrees dealing with Jerusalem and its Temple. Cyrus promulgated the first in 538 B.C. (Ezra 1:1-4), Darius I the second in 519 B.C. (Ezra 6:1-12), and Artaxerxes the third I in 457 B.C. (Ezra 7:12-26) and the fourth—the authorization given to Nehemiah to rebuild the wall of Jerusalem—in 444 B.C. (Neh. 2). Which of them is the decree mentioned by Gabriel?

1. *The Decree of Cyrus the Great in 538 B.C.*—Ezra 1:2-4 contains the text of Cyrus's edict that authorizes (1) the exiles to return to Jerusalem; (2) the rebuilding of the Temple; and (3) provisions for rebuilding the Temple. While the returnees joyfully celebrated the laying of the foundation of the Temple (Ezra 3:10-13), their zeal soon flagged when opposition arose (Ezra 4:1-4), and they suspended the building program (verse 24). The important point to note is that Cyrus's decree refers not to rebuilding the city but only the Temple. Since Daniel 9:25 clearly specified the reconstruction of the city of Jerusalem, the decree of Cyrus obviously does not qualify as the starting point for the 490-year prophecy.

2. *The Decree of Darius I in 519 B.C.*—According to Ezra 5:1, 2, Zerubbabel and Joshua, under the influence of the prophets Haggai and Zechariah, reinitiated the project of restoring the Temple several years

after it halted. However, when Tatnai, the governor of the region, saw what the Jews were doing, he wrote to Darius, asking him to verify the information he had received from the Jewish leaders (verses 3-5). After investigating the matter, which brought to light the decree of Cyrus, Darius issued another document confirming Cyrus's decree (Ezra 6:3-12). The decree of Darius is basically the same as Cyrus's edict. According to Ezra 6:15, the people of Jerusalem completed the Temple in March 515 B.C. Again, it is important to note that the decree of Darius referred only to the rebuilding of the Temple and not to the city of Jerusalem.

3. *The Decree of Artaxerxes I in 457 B.C.*—The decree of Artaxerxes included several important elements: 1. It granted permission to exiles willing to return to Judah to do so. 2. Ezra was to investigate the spiritual condition of the people in Judah, in order to bring their lives into harmony with the law of Moses. 3. Money received from the king and his counselors together with other funds would go to the support of the Temple in Jerusalem as well as for other perceived needs. 4. Temple and Temple personnel were exempted from taxes. 5. Ezra was to establish a judicial and civil system based on the Torah. The last point implied that the king restored the authority of the Jews to govern themselves on the basis of the law of God. However, the document says nothing directly about rebuilding the city.

Nevertheless, a number of interpreters believe that the decree of Artaxerxes, recorded in Ezra 7, was comprehensive enough to permit the rebuilding of Jerusalem. The text of a letter recorded in Ezra 4 indicates that the Jews under the leadership of Ezra did in fact rebuild the city. Ezra 4:7-23 states that a group of Persian officers wrote a letter to Artaxerxes recording their opposition to the rebuilding of Jerusalem by the Jews. "Let it be known to the king," they said, "that the Jews who came up from you have come to us at Jerusalem, and are building the rebellious and evil city, and are finishing its wall and repairing the foundations" (verse 12). This clearly indicates that Ezra must have understood his authority to include the restoration of Jerusalem.

The king's answer to the letter suggests that Artaxerxes had authorized the Jews to rebuild the city. If the rebuilding of the city had been unauthorized, the letters to and from Artaxerxes, recorded in Ezra 4, would have mentioned, if not stressed, the illegitimacy of the project. "The issue of the complaint is not the rebuilding of Jerusalem and its walls as being contrary to the law but the alleged harm that would come to emperor and empire were the city and its walls to be completely restored. The Jewish community is depicted as a potential rebel. It is not the rebuilding in itself which is depicted as rebellion. The king is advised that a rebuilt city would rebel and withhold tribute, custom, and toll."[2]

Artaxerxes' response, therefore, does not say that the rebuilding is illegal. It just mentions that he checked the history of Jerusalem and that it confirmed that the city had indeed been rebellious, and based on that finding, he ordered the project to stop (verses 19-21). The rebuilding was to be postponed to a future time to be determined by the king. In 444 B.C. he gave Nehemiah permission to finish rebuilding the city (Neh. 2).

4. *The Decree of Artaxerxes I in 444 B.C.*—In 444 B.C. Nehemiah, cupbearer to Artaxerxes I, received a report about the situation in Jerusalem that deeply shocked him (Neh. 1:3, 4). He requested and received permission from the king to go to Jerusalem to complete the rebuilding of the city and its walls, which, as we saw, Ezra had begun in 457 B.C. Arriving in Jerusalem, he managed to complete the walls in 52 days (Neh. 6:15), a further indication that much of the work of rebuilding the wall must already have happened under Ezra in 457 B.C.

The 70 Weeks

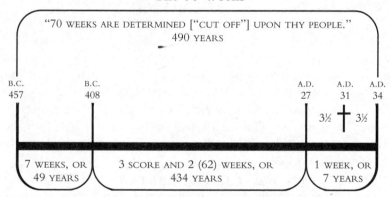

The 2300 Evenings and Mornings

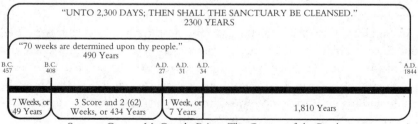

Source: George McCready Price, *The Greatest of the Prophets*
(Mountain View, Calif.: Pacific Press Pub. Assn., 1955), pp. 253, 254.

If we take 444 B.C. as the starting point for the 70-week prophecy, the end of the sixty-ninth week (483 years later) would place the Messiah in the year A.D. 40, a date well after the time of Christ. If, on the other hand, we regard 457 B.C. as the beginning of the 70 weeks, the Messiah appears in A.D. 27 (Jesus' baptism), and He is cut off (crucified) three and a half years later. Consequently 457 B.C. provides the best starting point for the 70-week and the 2300-evening-and-morning prophecies.

Explanation

Great changes had taken place since Daniel's last vision in chapter 8. Babylon no longer existed as a world empire, Medo-Persia now ruled the world, and Darius the Mede sat on the throne of Babylon. Daniel, though busy with affairs of state, wondered: What about the captivity of my people? When will they be able to return to Jerusalem?

Daniel's Prayer (Dan. 9:1-19)—Through confession and pleas for forgiveness Daniel sought to move God to permit His people's immediate release from captivity and the restoration of the sanctuary at Jerusalem. The answer to his prayer came quickly in the form of the angel Gabriel (verse 21), though what he heard was not the answer he had expected.

God still answers prayers in many and varied ways. They may include healing from sickness, the return of a lost son or daughter, or a raise in pay when least expected. And He hears prayers not only from sincere Christians, but also from earnestly praying non-Christians. Ranjit Singh was a Hindu in northern India. He and his wife had planted 2,500 cabbage plants in their garden, but without rain the continuing drought threatened to destroy their harvest. The Singhs had lost faith in the 300,000 gods of Hinduism on which they had called throughout their lives, but where could they go for help?

"Then Mr. Singh recalled hearing someone say that the God of the Christians was all-powerful. He talked it over with his wife, and they decided to pray to this unseen God for rain. 'If the God of the Christians hears our prayer and answers, then we will know that He is the true God,' Mr. Singh told his wife. For the first time in their lives the couple poured out their hearts to God for help. That night it rained. The next day the couple stood in amazement when they realized that the rain had fallen only on their cabbage patch and nowhere else in the village."[3] In time Mr. Singh and his wife accepted Jesus Christ as their Savior and became members of the Seventh-day Adventist Church.

A Heavenly Visitor—As we study the prophecy in Daniel 9 it is important that we remember the links between this and the previous chapter: 1. The same angel visited Daniel (verse 21). 2. Daniel recalled the former vision (verse 21). 3. Verse 23 repeats the command to Gabriel in Daniel 8:16 to give the prophet understanding of the vision. 4. The time element not explained in Daniel 8 is now the topic in Daniel 9 (verse 24).

Daniel 8 employs two words for "vision." One is *chazon* (verses 1, 2, 13, 15, 17, 26), and the other is *mareh* (verse 16, 26, 27). The first word refers to the vision as a whole; the second word focuses on the 2300-evening-and-morning time element. The angel had explained the animal and the little horn symbolism in chapter 8. What the prophet did not comprehend was the meaning of the "vision *[mareh]* of the evenings and mornings" (Dan. 8:26). "I was astonished by the vision *[mareh]*, but no one understood it" (verse 27). Therefore when Gabriel says in Daniel 9:23, "consider the matter and understand the vision," he does not use the word *chazon*, which refers to the vision as a whole, but employs *mareh*. This is an important link between chapters 8 and 9 that many have not recognized. One who does discern it is the Jewish commentator Rabbi Hersh Goldwurm, who, after citing the words of Gabriel in Daniel 9:23, "understand the vision," correctly explains that "this refers to Daniel's vision in chapter 8 in which the part which disturbed him so (verse 14) is characterized in verses 16-26 as a *mareh*."[4]

Daniel 9, therefore, is an integral part of Daniel 8. Gabriel in chapter 9 directs the prophet back to the unexplained part of chapter 8—the time prophecy of 2300 evenings and mornings, i.e., days. The link between these two chapters is underscored when Gabriel, after referring to the *mareh* vision (the 2300 days), tells Daniel that 70 weeks are "cut off" for the prophet's own people. Cut off from what? Obviously, from the 2300 days to which Gabriel had just been referring when he mentioned the *mareh* vision in Daniel 9:23.

While Bible versions generally translate the passage as "seventy weeks are determined for your people," Bible scholars acknowledge that the root meaning of the Hebrew word *chatak*, here translated "determined," is "to cut" or "divide." The extended meaning is "to determine" or "allot to." The word appears only in Daniel 9:24 in the Hebrew Bible, though it occurs in later Jewish writings predominantly as "to cut off." The 70 weeks are cut off from the 2300 years in Daniel 8:14 as a time period "assigned to the Jews with respect to their role as God's chosen people."[5]

70 Weeks (Dan. 9:24)—A footnote to Daniel 9:24 in the Revised Standard Version refers to "seventy weeks of years, or 490 years [i.e., 70 x

7 years], after which the messianic kingdom will come." That Jesus, the Messiah, did appear at the end of the 490-year period shows that we should understand the 70 weeks according to the year-day principle.

The passage lists six points in three pairs of what would happen during the 490 years. 1. "To finish the transgression" and "to make an end of sins." Some understand this to mean that God gave the Jewish people 490 years to decide whether they wanted to serve Him or themselves.[6] Others see it as a reference to the cross, where Jesus through His sacrifice brought to an end the broken relationship (transgression and sin) between God and humanity and restored us to God (2 Cor. 5:19).[7] 2. "To make reconciliation for iniquity" and "to bring in everlasting righteousness." The atoning sacrifice of Jesus Christ achieved this on the cross. 3. "To seal up vision and prophecy, and to anoint the Most Holy." For the Jews, vision and prophecy came to an end at the conclusion of the 70 weeks with the stoning of Stephen (Acts 6:12-7:60). It indicated the end of their special status as a nation.

What was so significant about the stoning of Stephen? Why was his martyrdom more important than that suffered by others at that time? Stephen's speech in Acts 7 parallels the prophetic "covenant lawsuit" speech. When the Holy Spirit came upon him, he received a vision of heaven. Thus by definition Stephen became a prophet at this point in time. When we look at his speech through the eyes of Old Testament prophets, it becomes another instance in which a divine prophet brings a covenant lawsuit against the representatives of God's covenant community. His death, therefore, is not just one more martyr's death. Stephen is the last of the Old Testament prophets to speak to the Jewish people as the elect people of God. But in stoning him they also silenced the prophetic voice addressed to them. "The prophets who followed Stephen were prophets *to the Christian church,* not to the nation of Israel."[8]

"To anoint the Most Holy." Temples were anointed to inaugurate their services (cf. Ex. 40:9ff.). The anointing of the heavenly sanctuary foretold in this verse points to the inauguration of Christ's priestly ministry in the heavenly temple after His ascension (Heb. 9:21ff.).

Messiah the Prince (Dan. 9:25-27)—From our study we learned that the starting point of the 70 weeks or 490 years, and therefore also of the 2300 prophetic days or literal years, was the year 457 B.C. "There shall be seven weeks and sixty-two weeks," Gabriel explained, "until Messiah the Prince" (verse 25). This time period has two sections, because during the first seven weeks, or 49 years (457-408 B.C.), the city of Jerusalem would undergo restoration. We know that Nehemiah completed the wall in 444 B.C., but since we have no historical records concerning Jerusalem from the end of the fifth century B.C., we cannot verify that in 408 the rebuilding was completed. Yet we have no reason to doubt that the number of years assigned in the prophecy for the task is correct.

The following 62 weeks, or 434 years (408 B.C.-A.D. 27), bring us to the year in which Jesus at His baptism became the Anointed One. At that time "God anointed Jesus of Nazareth with the Holy Spirit and with power" (Acts 10:38). It was then, and not before, that He became officially the Messiah. Following His baptism Jesus began preaching the gospel of the kingdom of God (Mark 1:14, 15) and confirming the covenant as Daniel 9:27 predicted. "When the early days of Christ's ministry are examined for a covenant-making or strengthening event, the presentation of the Sermon on the Mount stands out. Jesus took a selection of commandments from the old covenant and amplified or strengthened them; He did not do away with them (Matt. 5:21-48). Then He added to them His new commandments (Matt. 6:19-7:11)."[9]

In the middle of the last of the 70 weeks (A.D. 27-34), just as Gabriel had told Daniel, the Messiah was "cut off," or killed, and the daily ritual of sacrifice and offering lost its significance (Dan. 9:27)—type had met antitype. Another three and a half years later, with the stoning of Stephen in A.D. 34, the 490 years came to a close. "Thus with these terminal dates established, every subdividing date falls into place like a cog in a well-designed wheel meshing into its partner, predictions and events matching one another perfectly. All this is proof of inspiration, and proof also of the Messiahship of Jesus of Nazareth."[10]

In closing this section, we need to mention that the application of the seventieth week to the future, as dispensationalists do, is clearly impossible. Gabriel plainly declares that the Messiah will be "cut off" during the last week. In fact, he pinpoints it by saying in "the middle of the week." One consequence of the Messiah's death was going to be that "the people of the prince who is to come shall destroy the city and the sanctuary" (verse 26). In A.D. 70 the Roman legions under Titus fulfilled this prophecy.

Application

Some have called this chapter the backbone and crown jewel of prophecy. From Daniel's prayer to the confirmation of the covenant in Daniel 9:27, the chapter is bursting at the seams with practical lessons.

Unfortunately, because of the limitation of space we can touch on only one or two:

1. *His Prayer Life*—Daniel, the man for all seasons, was first and foremost a person of prayer. Neither his work as a statesman nor the "good life" at the luxurious Babylonian court could distract him from his daily communion with God. Are we always as faithful? Daniel's prayer included aspects of devotion, adoration (verse 4), confession (verses 5-14), thanksgiving (verse 15), and petition (verses 16-19).

Most of his prayer consists of a confession of sin. While Daniel led an exemplary life, he identified himself freely with his people and the stigma of their sins: "We have sinned and committed iniquity, we have done wickedly and rebelled" (verse 5); "righteousness belongs to You, but to us shame of face" (verse 7); and "we have not obeyed" (verse 10). He also acknowledged that God was acting justly in punishing them (verse 14). The prayer reaches its crescendo in verse 19: "O Lord, hear! O Lord, forgive! O Lord, listen and act!" And God did hear the prayer and acted by sending the angel Gabriel.

2. *The Messiah*—The focus of the prophecy in Daniel 9:24-27 is the Messiah, the time of His appearing, and His life and work, as well as His death. Yet no amount of intellectual understanding of this prophecy will benefit us unless we accept Jesus Christ as our personal Savior. This passage reveals a salvation not only from the consequences of sin, but from sin itself, and according to the New Testament, God offers it freely to all. However, we cannot purchase such a salvation—we can experience it only through our surrender to Jesus, who said: "Come to Me, all you who labor and are heavy laden, and I will give you rest" (Matt. 11:28).

---

[1] Leslie C. Allen, *Commentary on the Books of Joel, Obadiah, Jonah, and Micah* (Grand Rapids: W. B. Eerdmans, 1976), p. 370.

[2] Arthur J. Ferch, "Commencement Date for the Seventy Week Prophecy," in *Seventy Weeks, Leviticus, and the Nature of Prophecy,* p. 71.

[3] J. H. Zachary, "The God Who Sends Rain," in "Great Prayers and Pray-ers of the Bible," *Adult Sabbath School Bible Study Guide,* January-March 2001, p. 13.

[4] Hersh Goldwurm, *Daniel* (New York: Mesorah Publications, 1979), p. 258.

[5] *The Seventh-day Adventist Bible Commentary,* vol. 4, pp. 851, 852.

[6] W. H. Shea, *Daniel 7-12,* p. 57.

[7] A. Rodríguez, *Future Glory,* p. 60.

[8] Shea, *Daniel 7-12,* p. 59.

[9] Shea, "The Prophecy of Daniel 9:24-27," in *Seventy Weeks, Leviticus, and the Nature of Prophecy,* pp. 95, 96.

[10] George McCready Price, *The Greatest of the Prophets* (Mountain View, Calif.: Pacific Press Pub. Assn., 1955), p. 257.

CHAPTER 12

When Kings Go to War

The last vision in the book of Daniel has three sections: (1) the prologue in chapter 10; (2) the vision proper in Daniel 11:2-12:4; and (3) the epilogue in Daniel 12:5-13 that concludes not only the chapter but the whole book of Daniel. In this vision, given about two years after the return of the Jews from Babylon, God lifted the veil of history and showed Daniel some of the background to the conflict going on between the forces of good and evil. In Revelation 12:7-9 we find a similar picture, Michael and His angels fighting with Satan, the dragon, and his angels. Yet the outcome is never in doubt—Michael, i.e., Christ, overcomes Satan and delivers His people.

It is a scenario that has been and is being played out many times here on earth. During the unrest in Rwanda in 1994, Phodidas, a Tutsi Seventh-day Adventist, fled from Hutu militiamen. At the main road junction in Kigali a gang of men identified him as a Tutsi and ordered him to lie down next to a man they had recently killed. He refused and began to pray, "Lord, the time has come for You to show Your protection. Show them that I am Your servant and that You are my God." When one of the militiamen came with raised machete to kill him, Phodidas, with eyes wide open, prayed, "Lord, stop him in Jesus' name." As soon as he said it, the militiaman, who was now only about three feet from Phodidas, suddenly made a U-turn and walked back to where he had come from. The man seemed confused. Two other militiamen tried to kill him, but each time an unseen power stopped them. Phodidas knows that God had sent an angel to protect him. Some time later the militia miraculously sent him on his way.[1]

Information

In Daniel 11:2 Gabriel tells Daniel, "Behold, three more kings will arise in Persia, and the fourth shall be far richer than them all." At the time of the vision Cyrus (559–530 B.C.) was the ruling monarch. The next four kings were: Cambyses (530–522 B.C.), Gaumata or the False Smerdis (522 B.C.), Darius I (522–486 B.C.), and Xerxes (486–465 B.C.). The last one was the king who married Esther. When the Greeks destroyed his fleet at Salamis (480 B.C.) and defeated his army at Plataea (479 B.C.), the Persians gave up the idea of conquering Greece. One hundred fifty years later the Greeks under Alexander conquered Persia instead.

After Alexander's death four of his generals eventually divided the empire among themselves (see Dan. 7:6). Out of the divided Greek Empire arose two dynasties, the Seleucids and the Ptolemies, who became the kings of the north (the Seleucids in Asia Minor) and of the south (the Ptolemies in Egypt). The kings mentioned in Daniel 11:5-16 remained in power until the Romans took over their territories in the second and first centuries B.C.

The Abomination of Desolation—"The Hebrew *shiqqûṣ,* 'abomination,' is a common Old Testament term describing an 'idol deity' (e.g., Deut. 29:17; 2 Kings 23:24; 2 Chron. 15:8; Eze. 37:23). Such idol 'abominations' set up in the Temple at Jerusalem in Old Testament times were said to defile, or pollute, it (Jer. 7:30; Eze. 5:11). The Hebrew *shamem,* a form of which is translated 'desolation' (more literally, 'something that makes desolate'), is used of the devastation caused by an invading army (Jer. 12:11), a scene that creates a sense of horror in a person beholding it (Jer. 18:16). The Hebrew *pesha',* 'transgression,' in the parallel expression 'transgression of desolation' in Dan. 8:13, is used of acts of apostasy and rebellion against God (see Amos 2:4, 6; Micah 1:5)."[2]

The phrase "abomination of desolation" found in Matthew 24:15 derives from the book of Daniel, where the phrase, or variants of it, appear three times, namely Daniel 9:27; 11:31; and 12:11. In the Greek translation of the Old Testament (LXX) the three passages are almost word for word the same. However, Jesus in Matthew 24:15 refers back to Daniel 9:27, for it alone is in a context that speaks of the destruction of the city of Jerusalem. The Romans in A.D. 70 destroyed Jerusalem, burned the Temple, and in A.D. 135 erected a temple to Jupiter in its place.

Martin Luther identified the abomination of desolation in Daniel 11 with the Papacy and its doctrines and practices.[3] In view of the parallelism between Daniel 8:11, in which, as we saw, the little horn takes away the daily, and Daniel 11:31, in which again the daily is taken away but in addition the abomination of desolation is set up, it seems logical to conclude that the power that removes the daily is also the power that sets up the abomination of desolation. Hence, Seventh-day Adventists, as did Luther and many other Protestant commentators, believe that the Papacy and its teachings constitute the fulfillment of these prophecies in history.

Explanation

The last vision in the book of Daniel contains the most detailed prophecy of future events in the Old Testament. We do well to remember, therefore, that the great prophecies in Daniel are given according to the principle of repetition and enlargement. They begin either in the days of Babylon (Daniel 2 and 7) or Medo-Persia (Daniel 8 and 12), but they each climax in the establishment of the kingdom of God. Daniel 2, 7, and 8 all deal with the same powers. Chapter 7 enlarges Daniel 2, and Daniel 8 expands Daniel 7. We can expect therefore that the vision of Daniel 10-12 will enlarge the outline of Daniel 8.[4]

The Prologue in Daniel 10—The introduction to this chapter records that the events described took place in the third year of King Cyrus. His third year as king of Babylon would have been 535 B.C. Daniel, the passage informs us, has been mourning and fasting for three weeks. The text gives no reason for it, though from verse 14 we can infer that the future of his people must have concerned him. At the end of the three weeks Daniel, at the river Tigris, received a vision that revealed the conflict between the spiritual forces in the universe.

Daniel 10, probably more than any other passage in Scripture, exposes the invisible powers that rule and influence nations. In Scripture we read that spiritual beings carry out God's purpose in the physical world (Ex. 12:23; 2 Sam. 24:16), and the moral world (Luke 15:10), as well as in the political world. In this chapter, however, we learn not only that Israel had a spiritual champion to protect it as a nation and to watch over its interests (Dan. 10:21), but also that the nations opposed to Israel had their princes who were antagonistic toward those who watched over Israel. According to Ephesians 6:12, the "princes" of the pagan powers are "the rulers of the darkness of this age."

"In the annals of human history the growth of nations, the rise and fall of empires, appear as dependent on the will and prowess of man. The shaping of events seems, to a great degree, to be determined by his power, ambition, or caprice. But in the Word of God the curtain is drawn aside, and we behold, behind, above, and through all the play and counterplay of human interests and power and passions, the agencies of the all-merciful One, silently, patiently working out the counsels of His own will."[5]

The Vision (Dan. 11:2-12:4)—Modern critical scholarship views this chapter (11) as a description of the wars between the Seleucid (king of the north) and Ptolemaic (king of the south) rulers, culminating in the career of the Syrian king Antiochus IV Epiphanes, whom they see as the main actor in verses 21-45. Evangelical scholarship, generally, follows this outline, except that from verse 35 on some see the career of Antiochus Epiphanes foreshadowing the activities of the last-day antichrist, while others postulate a gap of many centuries between verses 35 and 36 and interpret the last 10 verses as applying only to a future antichrist.

Within the Seventh-day Adventist Church this chapter has received a variety of interpretations. The differences between the various authors concern primarily the question "At what points in the story do the Romans and the Papacy enter the picture?" *The Seventh-day Adventist Bible Commentary* and M. Maxwell see the Roman entry in verse 14; R. A. Anderson, G. M. Price, and W. H. Shea believe the Romans come on the scene in verse 16. J. B. Doukhan believes that the Romans appear briefly only in verse 4 and from verse 5 he has the Papacy as the king of the north until the end of the chapter. Maxwell applies verses 21-45 to the Papacy; Shea has the Papacy enter the story in verse 23; Price in verse 30; and *The Seventh-day Adventist Bible Commentary* and Anderson believe that not until verse 31 can we discern the activities of the Papacy. The interpretations of the individual verses differ accordingly.

Rather than attempting to decide which of the interpretations seems to be the right one, we will focus on those points in the story that are fairly clear and straightforward and that we can support by using the principle "scripture interprets scripture, one passage being the key to other passages."[6]

First, at the beginning of Daniel 11 the angel refers to Persian and Greek kings. The "mighty king" in verse 3, whose "kingdom shall be broken up toward the four winds" (verse 4), is clearly Alexander the Great. We see this supported by the parallelism with Daniel 8:8, in which Alexander is the large horn that shattered and in whose place "four notable ones came up toward the four winds of heaven." The four horns symbolize the Hellenistic kingdoms that emerged after the breakup of Alexander's empire.

The next clearly identifiable event is the death of the Messiah in Daniel 11:22. The word for "prince" in this verse is *nagîd*. The book of Daniel uses it in only one other place, namely, in Daniel 9:25 and 26. Elsewhere Daniel employs the word *sar* for "prince" (Dan. 8:11; 10:13, 20,

21, etc.). On linguistic grounds, therefore, the "prince of the covenant" in Daniel 11:22 is the same as "Messiah the Prince," who would "confirm a covenant with many for one week" (Dan. 9:25-27). Since Daniel 9:26, 27 and 11:22 obviously refer to the crucifixion of Christ under the Romans, the Roman Empire must enter the stage of history sometime prior to Daniel 11:22.

The third event that we can interpret by comparing scripture with scripture is the taking away of the daily and the setting up of the abomination of desolation in verse 31. The "taking away of the daily" is exactly the same expression used in Daniel 8:11, which we found referred to the removal of the intercessory ministration of Christ in the heavenly sanctuary through the papal priesthood. And the "abomination of desolation" represents the vast system of beliefs and practices that for more than 1,000 years led people away from the priestly ministry of Jesus. Thus the Papacy appears in this chapter (11) either with verse 31 or shortly before.

The fourth item that provides a chronological marker in the story is the expression "time of the end" in verse 40. The phrase appears only in the book of Daniel, once in the vision of Daniel 8 (verse 17) and four times in connection with Daniel's last vision (Dan. 11:35, 40; 12:4, 9). The visions of Daniel 8 and 11 both reach to "the time of the end," at which, according to Daniel 12:2, a resurrection takes place. Verse 4 indicates that just prior to the end of history people will study the Danielic visions just as the prophet himself did the 70-year prophecy (Dan. 9:2). And in the epilogue to the book of Daniel (12:5-13) the angel tells the prophet that "the words are shut up and sealed until the time of the end" (verse 9, RSV). Then knowledge of the visions will increase and people will understand their meaning (verses 4, 10). From history we know that in the nineteenth century, after the end of the 1260 years of Daniel 7:25, knowledge of the Danielic prophecies increased dramatically. "The prophetic days of Daniel had been understood as calendar years by only seven writers in the sixteenth century, and by only twelve in the seventeenth, but they were correctly understood by 21 of the 22 who wrote in the eighteenth, and by over 100 of the 109 who wrote on Daniel between 1800 and 1850."[7] It is reasonable, therefore, to conclude that the time of the end began with the fall of the Papacy in 1798. Therefore, we must seek the events from Daniel 11:40 onward in the time between the fall of the Papacy in 1798 and the resurrection at the end of time.

The fifth point that we can easily understand is the resurrection at the end of the vision (Dan. 12:2). The text states: "Many of those who sleep . . . shall awake," i.e., they shall be resurrected, some to eternal life and some to ever-lasting damnation. Clearly this cannot be the general resurrection at the Second Advent, when only the righteous will rise (1 Thess. 4:16, 17), nor the resurrection of the wicked 1,000 years later (Rev. 20:4-6). It must, therefore, be a special resurrection of some righteous and some wicked at the time of the seventh plague (Rev. 16:17, 18). This special resurrection will bring back to life all those who have died in the faith of the third angel's message. They "come forth from the tomb glorified, to hear God's covenant of peace with those who have kept His law. 'They also which pierced him' (Rev. 1:7), those that mocked and derided Christ's dying agonies, and the most violent opposers of His truth and His people, are raised to behold Him in His glory and to see the honor placed upon the loyal and obedient."[8]

These five points provide the basic outline for Daniel 11. All the other historical events mentioned in the chapter must fit into this chronological framework. That it is by no means an easy task we see indicated by the wide variety of interpretations among Seventh-day Adventist commentators.

Application

Daniel 11 teaches us that humanity has the freedom to oppose God. Although Satan and Christ sought to influence the mind of the king, nei-ther could force him. God displayed great condescension on His part to allow Himself to be "withstood"! But the same applies to each one of us. God decided to create human beings who could love Him of their own free will, and included in this freedom was the possibility of disobedience and resistance to His will. It does not mean that God is responsible for sin in our world—Satan, Adam, and Eve are. But as part of the free will God had to create the possibility of sin, otherwise there would not have been any true freedom. A father may give his son the key to the car, and the boy may drive the car into the next tree and kill himself. The father most cer-tainly did not intend this, but by handing his son the ignition key he also gave him the possibility to use the car as a deadly weapon.

This chapter also teaches us that the great controversy between good and evil is a real battle between the forces of good and evil, that angels are real, that there are both unfallen and fallen ones, and that they can influence human affairs. "While Satan was striving to influence the highest powers in the kingdom of Medo-Persia to show disfavor to God's people, angels worked in behalf of the exiles. The controversy was one in which all heaven was interested. Through the prophet Daniel we are given a glimpse of this mighty struggle between the forces of good and the forces of evil."[9]

Are we always aware of the presence of angels in our life, and how does it influence our words and actions?

---

[1] P. Ndamyumugabe, *Rwanda: Beyond Wildest Imagination,* pp. 48, 49.

[2] *Seventh-day Adventist Encyclopedia,* rev. ed. (Washington, D.C.: Review and Herald Pub. Assn., 1976), pp. 1, 2.

[3] See LeRoy E. Froom, *The Prophetic Faith of Our Fathers* (Washington, D.C.: Review and Herald Pub. Assn., 1948), vol. 2, pp. 277, 280.

[4] The prophecy in Daniel 9 is part of the explanation of the vision in Daniel 8.

[5] Ellen G. White, *Education* (Mountain View, Calif.: Pacific Press Pub. Assn., 1952), p. 173.

[6] White, *Evangelism,* p. 581.

[7] E. W. Marter, *Daniel's Philosophy of History,* p. 115; see also Froom, *Prophetic Faith,* vol. 2, pp. 528, 784, and vol. 3, p. 270.

[8] White, *The Great Controversy,* p. 637.

[9] White, *Prophets and Kings,* p. 571.

CHAPTER 13

The Time of the End

According to Daniel 12:1 the world's midnight is yet to come. It was a dark day when the Flood swept the antediluvian world into the pit. And it was a dark day when Jerusalem fell to the Roman armies and more than 1 million Jews perished. Fire and flood, war and famine, have all contributed to dark days in the world's history. But according to Daniel, one more dark day, "a time of trouble, such as never was," still lies ahead.

Obviously the devil is not going to give up without a struggle. The Dark Ages witnessed a time of trouble "such as never was" from persecution by the medieval church in which thousands of innocent Christian believers perished (Matt. 24:21, 22; Dan. 7:21, 25; 8:10, 13, 24). Just prior to the Second Advent there will come a time of trouble in which the seven last plagues will fall upon those who have oppressed God's people (Rev. 6:10, 11; 13:15; 16:1, 2). The seven last plagues originate in the temple in heaven, and holy angels will pour them on the earth (Rev. 15:6). Satan, no longer under restraint, will have "entire control of the finally impenitent," and "as the angels of God cease to hold in check the fierce winds of human passion, all the elements of strife will be let loose."[1]

Information

In recent years some Seventh-day Adventists have begun to apply the time periods in Daniel 12:5-13 to the future. Rejecting the traditional Adventist understanding that places the three and a half times, the 1290 and 1335 days, as prophetic periods in the past, they claim that we should understand these time periods as literal days still to come. According to one interpretation, the 1335 days begin with the national Sunday law (NSL) in America, and the three and a half times or 1260 days and the 1290 days with the universal Sunday law (USL).[2]

Such new proposals contain a number of problems that make such interpretations unacceptable:

1. They see the three and a half times or 1260 days in Daniel 7:25 and 12:7 as two different time periods in history, one in the past and one in the future. This interpretation violates one of the fundamental principles of biblical hermeneutics, namely, "scripture interprets scripture, one passage being the key to other passages."[3] If we discard this principle, prophecy becomes a wax nose that can be bent in any direction the interpreter wants it to go. As we have mentioned before, Scripture gives the prophecies of Daniel according to the principle of repetition and enlargement. We can clearly see this by looking at the four major prophecies in the book that all begin in the time of the biblical author and end with the Second Advent:

   a. Daniel 2: Babylon—Second Advent (stone kingdom)
   b. Daniel 7: Babylon—Second Advent (kingdom given to the saints)
   c. Daniel 8 and 9: Medo-Persia—Second Advent (little horn broken without hands)
   d. Daniel 10-12: Medo-Persia—Second Advent (resurrection)

These parallel prophecies cover essentially the same sweep of time from Daniel's day to the Second Advent. Each prophecy emphasizes different aspects of the time period, underlining the fact that we must interpret Daniel's prophecies in harmony with the "scripture interprets scripture" principle. Thus common elements in different chapters of the book must refer to the same things or events. For example, the little horn in Daniel 7 and 8 must represent the same historical power, not two different ones. If the "taking away of the daily" in Daniel 8:11 applies to events in the past, so must "the taking away of the daily" in Daniel 12:11, and if the three and a half times in Daniel 7:25 point to the past, so must the three and a half times in Daniel 12:7. To do otherwise makes a mockery of the "scripture interprets scripture" principle and leads to utter confusion.

2. Current reinterpretations see the passage in Daniel 12:5-13 as a new vision that contains time prophecies for the future. This view ignores the basic structure of Daniel's visions in which explanations always follow the visions themselves.

   a. Daniel 2: vision (verses 31-35), explanation (verses 36-46)
   b. Daniel 7: vision (verses 1-14), explanation (verses 15-27)
   c. Daniel 8, 9: vision (Dan. 8:1-12), explanation (verses 13-26; Dan. 9:24-27)

d. Daniel 10-12: vision (Dan. 11:2-12:4), explanation (Dan. 12:5-13)

While it is true that the vision in Daniel 11:2-12:4 is itself an explanation of the vision in Daniel 8, we must not overlook the fact that in Daniel 7, 8, and 10-12 the time prophecies are always situated within the explanation section, not in the visions themselves. In Daniel 7 the vision ends in verse 14, and the time prophecy appears in verse 25. Daniel 8 has the vision conclude in verse 12 and presents the time prophecy in verse 14. Finally, in Daniel 10-12 the vision ends in Daniel 12:4, and the time prophecies follow in verses 5-13. To interpret Daniel 12:5-13 as a new vision will destroy the literary structure.

3. This new view completely ignores the linguistic and grammatical connections between the vision in Daniel 11 and the explanation in Daniel 12. First, we need to emphasize that the vision concludes in Daniel 12:4 with the command to the prophet to "seal the book." Daniel 12:5-13 is an epilogue to the preceding vision and in a sense to the whole book. It is not a new vision with a different topic, but an explanation of certain elements in the vision of chapter 11. This is evident from the question in Daniel 12:6: "How long shall the fulfillment of *these wonders be?*" The Hebrew word *pala'* for "wonders" can be translated as "awesome events,"[4] or "something dreadful."[5] Since verse 5 does not refer to any dreadful or awesome events, "these wonders" can refer only to events in the vision in Daniel 11. The word *pala',* in fact, appears in Daniel 11:36, where it refers to the blasphemies spoken by the king of the north. Daniel 8:24 employs it when the verse speaks of the little horn destroying "fearfully *[pala']*." Furthermore, in Daniel 12:7 Daniel hears the words "and when the power of the holy people has been completely shattered, *all these things* shall be finished." Because he does not understand them, the prophet asks, "What shall be the end of *these things?*" (verse 8). Thus three times in Daniel 12:6-8 we have references to "these things/wonders." Each time they indicate the events of the vision in chapter 11. This clearly indicates that Daniel 12:5-13 is part of the vision of Daniel 11:2-12:4 and not a new vision.

Furthermore, we find a strong thematic and linguistic connection between the texts in Daniel 7:25 and 12:7:

Daniel 7:25: "[He] shall persecute the saints of the Most High. . . . The saints shall be given into his hand for a time and times and half a time."

Daniel 12:7: "He swore . . . that it shall be for a time, times, and half a time; and when the power of the holy people has been completely shattered, all these things shall be finished."

The shattering of the power of the holy people in Daniel 12:7 lasts for three and a half times and is the same as the persecution of the saints in Daniel 7:25 that also lasts for three and a half times, further evidence that the times in Daniel 12 refer not to the future but to the past.

4. Berry, one of the main proponents of this new view, begins both the 1260 and 1290 days in Daniel 12 with the universal Sunday law (see p. 110). The 1260 days, she believes, end with the universal death decree (UDD), while the 1290 days continue for another 30 days. She explains the extra 30 days as two 15-day time periods. The first 15 days are the "one hour" in Revelation 17:12 (360 divided by 24 is 15), and the second 15 days are the "one hour" referred to in Revelation 18:10. The scheme is an amazing mix of both literal and prophetic time. While she counts the first 1260 days as literal days, she regards the last 30 days of the 1290 as two prophetic hours that she interprets according to the year-day principle. This mixing of literal and prophetic time offers further evidence of the confusion in her concept.

The Daniel 12 Time Lines
(1260, 1290, 1335 Days)

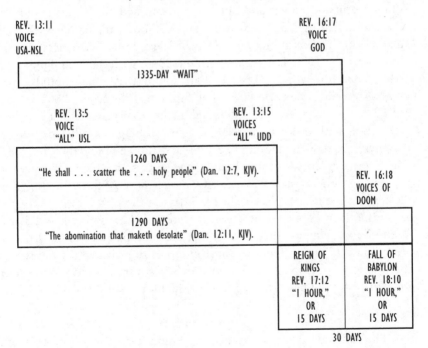

Source: Marian G. Berry, *Warning!* (Brushton, N.Y.: Teach Services, 1990), p. 154.

113

5. Finally, Berry's interpretation of the times in Daniel 12 is also against clear statements of Ellen White. In 1880 Mrs. White wrote: "I have borne the testimony since the passing of the time in 1844, that there should be no definite time set by which to test God's people. The great test on time was in 1843 and 1844; and all who have set time since these great periods marked in prophecy were deceiving and being deceived."[6] Now, it is true that Ellen White here speaks about date setting for the Second Advent, which the new view does not; nevertheless, we find no indication in her writings that any kind of prophetic time would play a role in the future.

In a letter from 1850 Ellen White mentions a Brother Hewit from Dead River who believed that the destruction of the wicked and the sleep of the dead was an abomination and that Ellen White was Jezebel. She then wrote, "We told him of some of his errors in the past, that the 1335 days were ended and numerous errors of his. It had but little effect."[7] Some believe that in her statement she places the 1335 days in the future. However, most generally understand the sentence to mean, "We told him of some of his errors in the past, [we told him] that the 1335 days were ended and [we told him] numerous errors of his." Otherwise we must ask, Why did Ellen White reprimand Hewit and not her husband and all the other pioneers who taught that the 1335 years were ended? For example, James White in an article in the *Review and Herald* in 1857 stated that "evidences are conclusive that the 1335 days ended with the 2300, with the Midnight Cry in 1844. Then the angel [Rev. 10:1-6] swore that time should be no longer."[8] In the same periodical Uriah Smith in 1863 stated: "We . . . date the 1290 days from the year 508; and as the 1335 days are spoken of in connection with these, no possible reason can be given why they do not commence at the same point. The 1290 and 1260 end together in 1798."[9] The fact that Ellen White nowhere argued against such statements supports the reading of her sentence as generally understood. At the same time it indicates that she herself placed the 1335 days in the past.

In summary, the evidence from Scripture and the writings of Ellen G. White do not support the concept that the time prophecies in Daniel 12 are still in the future. The Adventist interpretation that, in harmony with the historicist principles of interpretation, places these time prophecies in the past is still the best solution to the difficult texts in Daniel 12:11, 12.

Interpretation

The concluding portion of this long vision (Dan. 12:1-4) describes the final battle between the forces of God and those of Satan and the deliverance of the saints. When Christ appears in the clouds of heaven, He will free the righteous dead from their graves, where they have been held captive, and will deliver the living saints from death and the judgments of God in the seven last plagues. But deliverance comes only to those found written in the book of life, the register of the redeemed whose sins the blood of the Lamb of God has blotted out from the book of life.

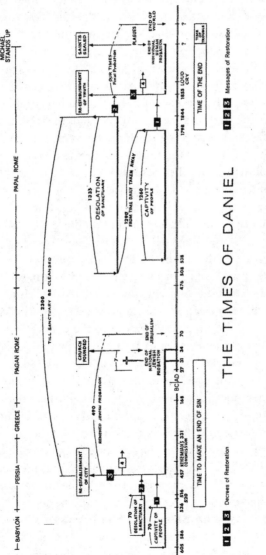

THE TIMES OF DANIEL

Ernest W. Marter, *Daniel's Philosophy of History* (Bracknell, Eng.: Newbold College, 1967), p. 119.

At That Time (Dan. 12:1)—"That time" is the period just mentioned in the preceding verse. The chapter division at this point is unfortunate, for the vision of chapter 11 ends in Daniel 12:4, not in Daniel 11:45. The first three verses of chapter 12 describe the conclusion of the conflict discussed at length in chapter 11.

Michael Shall Stand Up (Dan. 12:1)—Ancient Jewish writings described Michael as the highest of the angels and identified Him with the "angel of Yahweh" frequently mentioned in the Old Testament as a divine being. Such sources also claim that Michael was the angel who vindicated Israel against Satan's accusations at the heavenly tribunal.[10]

Michael, which means "who is like God," the One who stands up in defense of His people, is none other than Jesus Christ (1 John 2:1, 2; Heb. 4:14-16). When will Michael stand up? When He has completed His work in the heavenly sanctuary and the pre-Advent judgment is finished, He will stand up, and the door of mercy will close. "I saw that the anger of the nations, the wrath of God, and the time to judge the dead were separate and distinct, one following the other, also that Michael had not stood up, and that the time of trouble, such as never was, had not yet commenced. The nations are now getting angry, but when our High Priest has finished His work in the sanctuary, He will stand up, put on the garments of vengeance, and then the seven last plagues will be poured out."[11]

A Time of Trouble (Dan. 12:1)—The expression "a time of trouble such as never was" occurs in Daniel 12:1 and Matthew 24:21, one referring to the time of the end and the other to the Middle Ages. The phrase "such as has not been . . . no, nor ever shall be" in Matthew 24 is an idiom indicating the superlative nature of the event and should not be taken literally. For example, 2 Kings 18:5 tells us that Hezekiah "trusted in the Lord God of Israel, so that after him was none like him among all the kings of Judah, nor who were before him." Yet a few chapters further on, 2 Kings 23:25 describes Josiah as such a pious king that "before him there was no king like him, who turned to the Lord with all his heart, . . . nor after him did any arise like him." If we were to take the phrase literally, it could not be true of both kings. Thus expressions as "such as never was . . . no, nor ever shall be" or "there was none like him, not before him nor after him" are idiomatic. In the case of the "time of trouble" the idiom refers to the magnitude and intensity of this time period.

Many of Those Who Sleep . . . Shall Awake (Dan. 12:2)—The text says "many" shall be resurrected, some to eternal life and some to everlasting damnation. As already mentioned in the previous chapter, the fact that both good and bad will arise indicates that it cannot be the general resurrection at the Second Advent. Rather, it is a special resurrection of some righteous and some wicked at the time of the seventh plague (Rev. 16:17, 18).

"Graves are opened, and 'many of them that sleep in the dust of the earth . . . awake, some to everlasting life, and some to shame and everlasting contempt' (Dan. 12:2). All who have died in the faith of the third angel's message come forth from the tomb glorified, to hear God's covenant of peace with those who have kept His law. 'They also which pierced him' (Rev. 1:7), those that mocked and derided Christ's dying agonies, and the most violent opposers of His truth and His people, are raised to behold Him in His glory and to see the honor placed upon the loyal and obedient."[12]

"Many Shall Run To and Fro" (Dan. 12:4)—This is a Hebrew idiom for "searching" (cf. Jer. 5:1; Amos 8:12; Zech. 4:10, KJV). When God's Spirit would unseal the book of Daniel after the commencement of the time of the end, knowledge regarding the prophecies in the book of Daniel would increase. From history we know that this is indeed what happened in the nineteenth century, following the end of the 1260 years in 1798 (see p. 114).

The Epilogue (Dan. 12:5-13)—Daniel is still by the river Tigris, where he was in Daniel 10:4. Now he overhears a conversation between two heavenly figures and eventually joins in it. The passage parallels Daniel 8:13, 14 in several ways. Both take place beside a river, both involve two anonymous heavenly beings, and both deal with the question "How long?"

"How long shall the fulfillment of these wonders be?" (Dan. 12:6). As indicated previously, this question refers back to the vision in chapter 11. Gabriel had given Daniel a long explanation to help him understand what will happen to God's people (Dan. 10:14). Now two other heavenly beings appear, and one of them, for Daniel's information, asks Michael, the man clothed in linen, a question. The answer in Daniel 12:7 defines the time of the end as that which follows the 1260 years of papal supremacy and persecution. "In this answer Daniel was actually given the other half of the answer to the question asked by these same celestial attendants in 8:13. That question concerned the trampling under foot by the papal power of *both* sanctuary and host. In 8:14 the answer given was that the *sanctuary* would be trampled down till 1844. Now the answer is given that the *host* will be trampled down till 1798. And in the ensuing enquiry by Daniel and answer by Michael will be given the relationship between these two periods."[13]

117

1. *1290 days* (Dan. 12:11)—"And from the time that the daily sacrifice is taken away, and the abomination of desolation is set up, there shall be one thousand two hundred and ninety days." The book of Daniel mentions the taking away of the *tamîd* (the daily) three times:

Daniel 8:11: no specific time connected with it

Daniel 11:31: again, no specific time or date given

Daniel 12:11: "from the time . . . one thousand two hundred and ninety days"

It is important to note the parallelism between Daniel 11:31 and 12:11.

Daniel 11:31: "Forces shall be mustered by him [king of the north], and they shall defile the sanctuary fortress; then they *shall take away the daily sacrifices, and place there the abomination of desolation.*"

Daniel 12:11: "And from the time that the *daily sacrifice is taken away,* and the *abomination of desolation is set up,* there shall be one thousand two hundred and ninety days."

The two texts clearly refer to the same events in history. Now, if Daniel 11:31 speaks of the past, so must Daniel 12:11. And if they don't have in mind the same event, the principle "scripture interprets scripture" becomes irrelevant.

In Daniel 8:11 we saw that "the daily" represents Christ's intercessory ministry that the work of the priests through the Mass and the confessional usurped. By sacrificing Christ anew in every Mass, the Papacy has erased Christ's heavenly ministry from human thought. How long has this been going on? In May 1998 Pope John Paul II issued his pastoral letter *Dies Domini,* in which he called for Sunday laws. In the same letter he speaks about the attendance at Sunday Mass. Early in the history of Christianity, he says, people had to be reminded to attend Mass. Sometimes the church had to resort to specific canonical precepts: "This was the case in a number of local Councils from the fourth century onwards (as at the Council of Elvira of 300, which speaks not of an obligation but of penalties after three absences) and most especially from the sixth century onwards (as at the Council of Agde in 506). These decrees of local Councils led to a universal practice, the obligatory character of which was taken as something quite normal."[14]

Here the pope says that particularly from the beginning of the sixth century on, universal statutes made it obligatory for the people to attend Mass. As Seventh-day Adventists we also say that in the sixth century the daily was taken away and the abomination of desolation was established. We begin the 1290 years with 508. Why? Primarily because deducting 1290 from 1798, which we understand to be the end of the 1260 and 1290 years, brings us to 508.

What happened in 508? In 496 Clovis, king of the Franks, became a Roman Catholic. All the other Germanic tribes who had dismantled the Roman Empire were Arians and therefore opposed to the pope in Rome. Clovis defeated the Visigoths and became the first civil power to join up with the rising church of Rome. Tradition has, therefore, called France the oldest daughter of the Roman Catholic Church.

"After his great victory over the Goths in 507 . . . Clovis came to Tours, probably in the middle of 508, to hold a victory celebration. . . . According to Gregory of Tours, the ceremony began outside the walls of Saint Martin. In the cathedral church Clovis donned a purple tunic and chlamys, a vestment that was part of the usual uniform of imperial officials. He added a diadem, mounted a horse, and rode in procession into the city up to the cathedral, tossing gold and silver to the inhabitants who lined the streets."[15] Some have seen the incident as the "the first German coronation of an emperor."[16] The joining of the civil and the religious powers (Franks and the Papacy) at that time was an important step in "setting up the abomination of desolation," which refers to the unscriptural teachings of the Papacy and their enforcement through the union of church and state. It is one of the ironies of history that France, the power that helped the Papacy at the beginning of the 1290 years, was the same power that brought about its demise at the end of this time period when Napoleon in 1798 had Pope Pius VI taken prisoner.

2. *1335 days* (Dan. 12:12)—"Blessed is he who waits, and comes to the one thousand three hundred and thirty-five days." The passage mentions no specific event for the beginning of the 1335 days. The context, however, seems to imply that it began at the same time as the 1290 days. If that is correct, the 1335 days ended in 1843-1844 at the time of the preaching of the first angel's message. (It was also the last year of the 2300-year prophecy that runs from the fall of 1843 to the fall of 1844.)

The book of Daniel does not connect the 1335-day prophecy with the activity of the little-horn power. Rather it relates it to a special blessing for those who live at the end of that time period. Another blessing for the time of the end appears in Revelation 14:13: "Blessed are the dead who die in the Lord from now on."

Indeed, blessed were those who lived at the time of the Advent expectancy when the first angel's message spread through Europe and America. And blessed are those who die in the faith of the third angel's message in the time of the end, for they will take part in the special resurrection that will precede the Second Advent and the first resurrection.

Application

In chapter 12 we meet the soul winners, that is, "those who turn many to righteousness" (verse 3). It is also the place in which we find the clearest Old Testament text about the resurrection (verse 2). Here also the book of Daniel indicates the conclusion of the great controversy between Christ and Satan through the word "deliverance" (verse 1).

Righteousness—"Those who are wise shall shine like the brightness of the firmament, and those who turn many to righteousness like the stars forever" (verse 3). Righteousness in Scripture refers both to character and standing. In reference to character, a righteous person has a correct relationship with God and lives in conformity with His law (1 John 2:3, 4), which is a transcript of His character. Relative to standing, righteousness is a state of divine acceptance and approval and freedom from condemnation (Rom. 8:1). Yet how can sinful humans find acceptance by a holy God? How can sinners be right with their Maker? It is only by the substitution of a righteous and divine person in place of sinful human beings that the latter, on their acceptance of Him, can be regarded as righteous in the eyes of divine law. "If you give yourself to Him, and accept Him as your Savior, then, sinful as your life may have been, for His sake you are accounted righteous. Christ's character stands in place of your character, and you are accepted before God just as if you had not sinned." [17]

Resurrection—The resurrection at the end of time is one of the pillars of the Christian faith. Christ's resurrection is the object of our faith, for without it, Paul declares, our faith is futile (1 Cor. 15:17). Our own resurrection is the object of our hope (Acts 23:6). Every time we bury a loved one, the hope of the resurrection gives us strength and courage to carry on (1 Thess. 4:14, 18). It was this hope that enabled the martyrs to face the rage of their persecutors, and it is this hope that has sustained millions of others who have suffered for their faith ever since.

Deliverance—Scripture always remembers God as the one who delivered Israel from the bondage in Egypt (Ex. 3:8; Acts 7:34). He delivered them from the Midianites (Judges 8) and the Philistines (2 Sam. 5:25). The Lord delivered Jerusalem from the Assyrians (2 Kings 19:35) and His people from Babylon (Ezra 1:3). In the book of Daniel we hear of the deliverance of Shadrach, Meshach, and Abednego from the fiery furnace (Dan. 3) and of Daniel's deliverance from the lions' den (Dan. 6). And in Daniel 12:1 we read again of God delivering His people—this time not from the clutches of evil potentates or the mouths of lions, but from Satan himself. Long have the saints of the Most High been pilgrims and strangers in a foreign land. They have been persecuted and martyred, and from their graves their blood has been crying out to God for deliverance (Rev. 6:9-11). When the King of kings descends upon a cloud, at last the day of their deliverance will have come.

---

[1] E. G. White, *The Great Controversy,* p. 614.

[2] Marian G. Berry, *Warning!* (Brushton, N.Y.: Teach Services, 1990), p. 154.

[3] White, *Evangelism,* p. 581.

[4] E. Lucas, *Daniel,* p. 296.

[5] L. Koehler and W. Baumgartner, *The Hebrew and Aramaic Lexicon of the Old Testament,* rev. ed. (Leiden: E. J. Brill, 1996), p. 927.

[6] James White, *Life Sketches: Ancestry, Early Life, Christian Experience, and Extensive Labors of Elder James White, and His Wife, Mrs. Ellen G. White* (Battle Creek, Mich.: Steam Press, 1880), p. 222.

[7] Ellen G. White, *Manuscript Releases* (Silver Spring, Md.: E. G. White Estate, 1990), vol. 6, p. 251.

[8] James White, "The Judgment," *Review and Herald,* Jan. 29, 1857, p. 100.

[9] Uriah Smith, "Short Interviews With Correspondents," *Review and Herald,* Feb. 24, 1863. I am indebted to Alberto R. Timm for the Ellen White and pioneer sources. He published an article on the topic in Portuguese under the title "Os 1290 e 1335 dias de Daniel," *Ministeria* (Brazil), May-June 1999, pp. 16-18.

[10] See Talmud, Yoma 37a; Midrash Rabbah, on Genesis 18:3 and Exodus 3:2 and 12:29.

[10] Ellen G. White, *Early Writings* (Washington, D.C.: Review and Herald Pub. Assn., 1945), p. 36.

[12] White, *The Great Controversy,* p. 637.

[13] E. W. Marter, *Daniel's Philosophy of History,* p. 115.

[14] Pope John Paul II, *Dies Domini* (May 31, 1998), section 47, available at the Vatican Web site: www.vatican.va/holy_father/john_paul_ii/apost_letters/documents/hf_jp-ii_apl_05071998_dies-domini_en.html.

[15] Herwig Wolfram, *The Roman Empire and Its Germanic Peoples* (Berkeley, Calif.: University of California Press, 1997), pp. 221, 222.

[16] *Ibid.,* p. 222.

[17] Ellen G. White, *Steps to Christ* (Mountain View, Calif.: Pacific Press Pub. Assn., n.d.), p. 62.